BEYOND THE BLO(

"A powerful, moving, inspiring account of one woman's descent into mystery and magic. By expressing her own unique journey Michelle offers a guiding hand that leads others to the deep wisdom of Womankind."

Kristoffer Hughes, author of *From the Cauldron Born*

"Michelle Axe's Blood Red Cave is a place of both challenge and sanctuary. Drawing on her personal experience of the sacred feminine which she has been exploring since childhood, Michelle skilfully takes her reader by the hand and helps her journey through a series of caves that contain the feminine mysteries. Michelle's writing is direct and clear, her insights wise and informed, her visualizations and rituals tested and effective. Where she uncovers sacred truths with poetic language (a true bardic gift) she can reach stunning heights of awareness and understanding. *The Blood Red Cave* is a book of inner travel and spiritual development, a book to awaken women everywhere to honour their sacred role in the world, a book to help men respect and understand their inner feminine, a book to keep by the bedside, to use and treasure."

Claire Hamilton, author of *Tales of the Celtic Bards* and *Maiden, Mother: Crone, Voices of the Goddess*

"This is a wonderful book, which 'spoke' to me, coming from a place of authentic truth. It is filled with deep understanding and connection to the old ways, while fully being a book of the present time. It is filled with significance and power for what it means to be a woman.

It begins with a deep understanding of the significance of the cave to the people of our ancient land and gently leads us to a deeper understanding of the old ways that are always part of us when we become open to them. This book helps us to do just that, and opens the way to a deeper knowledge of ourselves.

Michelle writes with clarity and wisdom, born of her own life's experiences and personal stories. She takes us on a journey deep inside ourselves connecting us to a way of life that embraces the elemental, the mystical, the magical and includes significant personal ritual. Through a series of shamanic journeys into the caves of our inner selves, the book creates a bridge, a gateway, a portal that helps us find a greater understanding our selves and so that we become more fully aware of our power in the present moment and in these present times.

This is a book to read many times, to soak up the teachings, to follow the exercises and journeys, to learn from and be set into motion by. It is rich and overflowing with insight and warmth, a book that inspires our reconnection to the sacred feminine, and our full and whole selves. It is filled with healing and empowerment and I will be buying many copies for my women friends!"

Glennie Kindred, author of *Letting in the Wild Edges*,
Earth Wisdom, *Tree Ogham* and *Herbal Healers*

BEYOND
THE BLOOD RED CAVE

Michelle Axe

www.learbooks.co.uk

This first edition published by:
Lear Books
Windrush House
High Tor West
Earl Shilton
Leics
LE9 7DN
UK

Cover design by Anna Franklin
Cover illustration by Jamie Joel Blackwater www.paganportraits.co.uk
Author photograph by Sally Trendel

ISBN 978-1-907614-13-2

Printed in England by Booksprint.

Dedication

For my children Lucci and Crispy and Charlotte, my child in the spirit realm. To all of the amazing, talented, strong, eccentric and beautiful women that have shared their lives with me and in doing so helped to shape mine.

Acknowledgments

There are so may people to thank for helping me on this writing journey: Thorney Davis – an inspiration who is greatly missed – always told me I would write this book, she was right and I know she still walks with me in spirit; Kris Hughes who over the years has nagged me, pushed me and supported me through this processes, bless love, but we got there in the end; all my friends – Karen Iles, Fiona Ross Scott and Sue Matthews to name but a few who stood by me through thick and thin. Then there are all of the wonderful talks I have had with Bob Trubshaw. To my wonderfully talented partner Jamie Joel Blackwater I want to say thank you for your absolute belief in me, for your love, support and wisdom which has made all of this possible. Finally to Anna Franklin who, despite the complications of editing a book written by a dyslexic, has been fantastic in her support and patience in guiding me through the whole experience.

Michelle Axe
May 2013

CONTENTS

The Oak
I asked the Oak which way to turn
He said "Listen my child, listen and learn
Listen to the wind and the rain
Listen to your heart and question."

"Question what?" I asked straight back
He smiled and answered
"You're needed to learn
Your need to live
Your very existence
So seek it with urgent persistence."

The Oak continued
"Live with the seasons
Live with the land
And all that you ask
You will find first hand

Knowledge is your food
The earth is your blood
Stop starving yourself
And feed."

Beneath the ancient oak that spread its outstretched arms in search of the sun, a small child sat alone, her face stained and wet, her left knee bloody from her fall, but underneath the oak she felt safe and comforted. Why was not clear to her, but that old oak was wise and offered its protection without question and smiled upon its latest charge.

The day passed gently and the cool evening breeze rustled through the old oaks leaves. The child had remained locked in her thoughts for most of the day, but now she looked up into his caring gnarled branches and the oak knew his time had arrived. With ease and deliberation he shook the lowest of his branches, allowing one solitary acorn to drop into the child's lap. A precious gift, he thought to himself and so appropriate.

"Pick it up dear one" he whispered, "Pick it up little one, go ahead don't be afraid". The child hesitated, but the oak had been so kind and so picking the acorn from her skirt she held it tightly in her hand...and so I sat and I wondered for a very long time about the lesson the Old Oak was teaching me...

Welcome to the Blood Red Caves, a place of coming together, of learning and of celebrating all that it means to be us, the blessed sacred feminine and what it can and often means to be a woman. The Red Caves are a place that for millennia generations of women before us gathered, created, understood, embraced and bled for their magic, mysteries and their lives. This sacred place was not just an important, but an essential part of their lives, an intrinsic part of them as individuals

FOREWORD
Reconnection

I live my life honouring the Old Ways. The true essence of my spirituality and craft is the understanding that it is ultimately about survival, the preservation of self, family, friends, community and tribe, understanding how to utilise all the natural gifts and tools that you are born with and those that you develop along your life path, so that the life journey is both meaningful and an honest reflection of who you are. It is about being the best that you can be in any given situation, regardless of the perceptions and demands of others - in other words, *to know truth, love truth and to maintain truth*. This is the spirit and physicality of all life and for me is depicted in the symbolism of the *Awen* itself with its beautiful three rays, and in the eternal Tree of Life. These powerful emblems represent, for me, the totality of life, within a three realm depiction and with an important meaning of mind, body and spirit and of land, sea and sky.

If we look, for example, at the tree, to explain this concept we recognise the characteristics of a tree as being roots, trunk, and branches or canopy in its most simplistic form:

Roots:
The roots are the hidden aspect, but that which nourishes us and keeps us fed and strong. They can be seen as the hidden wisdoms and knowledge that sustain us and are passed down generation to generation. Do we not often need to feel rooted, even using that very expression? The

roots represent our mind, that which cannot easily seen, but represents absolutely what is done by thought, dream, aspiration and intellect

Trunk:
As we move up the tree the roots become the trunk, strong, tough and weathering all storms, flexible and always growing. This represents our bodies, what can be seen in our features as well as the physical aspects of our bodies. The trunk is what holds us up. It is our dependability, our stability, our strength and the practical things that are required within day to day life.

Branches:
We are now up into the branches of the canopy of the tree, the spirit of who we are reaching for the sky with no limitations and no barriers. Our spirit of independence and self are held here. Our aspirations, our hopes and fears flow along the branches. We are as complex and as beautiful as the tree itself, with many branches stretching up and out, breathing in the air, feeling the way as we go as we are held by the strength of our body the trunk and nourished and feed by the anchor that is our roots.

Over the years I have found that it is predominantly the yew that is considered the Tree of Life. If we look to understand what it is that it represents we find that the meaning of the Tree of Life is in fact us or more specifically 'I', as in 'I' am an individual, 'I' *am* the Tree of Life. For example;:

- Brythonic/Celtic – The World Tree is the yew, its ancient name being *Eioh* of which the translation is 'I'.
- Anglo Saxon – The World Tree is the yew, its ancient name being *Ih* which means 'I'.
- Norse: The World Tree is the yew, its ancient name being *Igg Drasal* of which the translation is 'The Carrier of I'.

- Brythonic Welsh – The World Tree is the yew, its ancient name being *Yodden* of which the translation is 'I'.

I think you might see a picture emerging and those examples I have chosen are not exclusive: we can find the same understanding of 'yew' within Germanic and Old Irish/Gaelic.

Eventually we should all come to see that the truth is 'I', the individual, the person, and the living entity.

Many of us may not have the customs and teachings of our ancestors as commonplace in our lives any more. We may not always feel held, respected, listened to or even always understood, but we as women still need to be nurtured and held and taught the beauty and power that is womanhood and the sacred feminine. Consequently, it is my contention that we still need the Blood Red Caves - both seen and unseen. Within the pages of this book we have an opportunity to explore the magic, craft and tradition of the sacred feminine within the magical and spiritual practices of women based in the indigenous tradition of the very ancient and sacred 'Isle of the Mighty'.

As individuals, and as women, we all have unique experiences and life stories that have helped to shape us and made us the people we are today. We all need time and space to reflect on our own lives, to take ownership and control of the many issues that have made us into the unique individuals that we are. To understand others we must first look at and understand ourselves - that is part of the journey and essential to our personal development, health and wellbeing.

However, this book is a reflection of my personal experiences, my understanding of my craft and spirituality. All I have decided to share can be viewed as a window (if slightly in need of cleaning from time to time), showing how I have used and implemented the theory into practice. This in turn has enabled me to develop on my personal life's journey with the aid and support of my craft and magical understanding. I will say, however, that most of my experiences have been born out of the personal twists and turns that my life has taken. I would suggest that this would be no different for the majority of us. Consequently, my personal journey has incorporated the teachings and lessons that I have learned throughout my life, particularly in the way in which experiences and knowledge have impacted upon my life and those around me. I have focused on some of the more challenging and critical turning points in my life, because it is at these points that the most noticeable changes, understandings and insights were gained, and perhaps this is a truth that all of us can recognise in our own lives.

Compared with most I had a fairly bohemian upbringing, with my father at sea for most of my childhood, so my sister, brother and I grew up with our mother in what I remember as a noisy and creative home. It was the era of hot lazy summers, wide-brimmed hats, droughts, three day weeks and national strikes, and I refer to them lovingly as my Fleetwood Mac days. Most of our days were spent out of doors, playing with the fairies that lived in our garden, making lotions and herbal potions, and grass houses from the cuttings in the greens around our house, along with dens lovingly made with blankets, sticks and cardboard boxes.

I always felt wild and free as a child, barefoot for the most part with my hair long, tangled and flying in the wind. I was fed on stories of the fair folk and of magic, spoon-fed on the legends and folklore relating to Great Britain and our extraordinary and impressive Celtic heritage, the rich history of the gods and goddesses that were forgotten by most.

My playground was the remains of an ancient oak and elm forest, the expansive common given to the people of Kingswood by King John in the Magna Carta, and the disused Victorian railway with its very steep embankments.

We often went foraging, be it for nuts, mushrooms, berries, herbs and specific greenery. My mother always took us, along with half the neighbourhood children, and what she taught me was the start of my absolute love of hedgerow gathering and associated craft. My grandma introduced me to the sacred landscape and ensured that I understood the relevance and importance of the ancient stone circles, particularly Avebury and Stonehenge and, along with my grandpy, instigated my understanding of the connection of everything in the natural cycle of things, ensuring that I recognised the importance of honouring the spirits of place. This we did every full moon, leaving food offerings out for the fairies and the spirits of the garden and land, a tradition I continued in later years with my own children. Why? Well because as we all know, nothing is gained without sacrifice.

I was sent my first tarot at the age of twelve (I still don't know who by, but think it might have been my grandma) and I have continued to develop the divinatory side of my nature ever since.

Over the years I have been supported by other very strong women: Thorney for herbal knowledge and insight into nature, history and journey work; Aunty Anne for all things witchy and Pagan and connecting me with the sacred landscape, and Bonnie for glamour, creativity and confidence. They are all amazing women in their own right, and along with my mother and my grandmother I know I have been blessed…and sometimes cursed.

My rites of passage came at age sixteen, a horrific affair for a teenager, when my grandma required me to 'get naked' with her in a public sauna that she had hired for the day. She told me about her life, her hopes, her fears and the things she felt were important to know. It was an amazing, humbling experience, but not one that I appreciated or truly understood until I was a grown woman and had experienced more of what life had to offer and take away. Now it is one of my most treasured memories and I know it will stay with me until it is my turn to join her again in the Summerlands and take my place with the rest of my loved ones.

For all my life my craft has intertwined and woven itself around and through all that I am and all that I do. It is not a conscious thing: I do not need to think about it on a mundane level, it just is. The craft, magic and spirituality that I practice is as it always has been: locality specific, time specific and relevant to the now. I walk between the worlds on so many levels. By definition I practice an indigenous shamanic tradition that is probably as old as the hills themselves. So much can be said to have been lost, but I would argue that in reality it is very difficult to lose something that is a natural part of who and what we are.

Today, I am known primarily as a Druid but I could just as easily be labelled a witch. As usual it's always about perspective, location and is, without doubt, time specific. For my part, I love both titles and will use either or both, because I am all these things and more. A label is just that, a label; it does not and should not define the totality of who and what you are. I am an ordained priestess of Anglesey and a member of the Anglesey Druid Order, I am joint head and founder of the Order of Gwyddon, but I am also a solitary practitioner. My Gods are personal to me and wherever I am, so are they.

Through my twenties and thirties I immersed myself in the raising of my children. As they have grown they have had the same freedom that I had to learn and explore. I have not imposed my beliefs or my way of life, though obviously they were brought up in a home that honours the Old Ways. In my career I worked with girls and young women in marginalised communities, drug and alcohol dependants and those at risk of sexual exploitation and domestic abuse. During this time I also developed workshops in ritual and everyday magical practice and hedgerow crafts. My divinatory practice grew and eventually I incorporated it in my teaching. In recent years I have been involved in the organisation and running of camps and ceremonial/ritual weekends. I write poetry and songs and love to sing and play my guitar around the fire with friends. I am a glass artist, a sculptress and an author.

However, the true essence of my spirituality and craft is in the intrinsic understanding that it is ultimately about being the best that you can at any given time. It is about striving to reach your potential without fear of the necessary lessons, without fear of the knocks and failures which teach us the most about ourselves whilst we are on the journey to reaching that goal - which is about living life itself. It is also about survival, preservation of self, family, friends, community and tribe. It is about all of the above and yet so much more. However, most importantly, it is about recognising and understanding the need to 'sing the song of self'.

Blessing of the Blood Red Cave

Welcome circle of women
Welcome to the Blood Red Cave
This is a place of personal craft and of the collective mysteries in
honour of Womankind and our place within the sacred feminine
Know that you walk in the footsteps of the ancestors

Your blood is their blood
Your bone is forged from their bone
You are the fire that shines down through the ages
The keeper of ancestral knowledge passed down

We call to the spirits of this place, seen and unseen
To the elemental forces that hold this space
Protected and in balance whilst we weave
We call to the great Goddess, seen and unseen
Within and without as we journey into the womb of all we were,
all that we are
And all that we are yet to become.

As with all good stories it is always considered best and even polite to start at the beginning, yet so much time has passed that I am unsure as to when that truly was. But fear not my friends, time may have turned my physical body to dust, but my life force remains fast and has forgotten nothing of what has been, nor of what manifested as a consequence.

I am of the Gwyddon, who were known as the 'dream weavers', the 'walkers between the worlds', we who carried the law of the Gods and of man and sang our history into the mists of time; we who were the teachers and the healers and the oracles, the priests, the watchers and the magical workers. Protectors and warrior cast we walked with the knowledge that ensured the survival of the people.

Know me, for my breath is the whisper on the breeze, my heartbeat the pulse that awakens the land, my tears the sea, rivers and streams that quench your thirst. I am both seen and unseen, within and without. I am all things. I am nothing. I am part of you, and yet in truth but a distant memory hidden deep within your being. You know me as I you and yet it can not be denied that we are strangers. I am your past as I am your future and this is your story as much as it was mine.

Ultimately, does any of this matter? I ask you as I answer, yes and no. How much and in what order is down to you, that is your truth. My path has always been clear in this matter and my shadow brings me to you so that you may understand and find the key to yours. Make no mistake my little piglets, this is, with out doubt, a journey of Truth. For your part, well… you need only decide your own truth but in doing so allow others the same courtesy. For your truth may not be another's and there, dear friend, lies the problem that shook our world and by definition helped shape yours.

So I will begin nonetheless and put my trust in the words that I shall write allowing the facts to unravel themselves in their true order. I am sure you will understand that this was ever the way of the Gwyddon, regardless of the fanciful tales and misnomers that have been written about us since. So in one of our great traditions I will trust you to come to your own conclusions.

When the world was still considered young and the Gods of this land were known, loved and even feared, a blanket of darkness descended to cover us all. We, as a mighty nation of differing tribes, colourful in our languages, customs and traditions were thriving. We were connected with the greater world and understood the way and the meaning of the secret spiral of life, but when the might of the Romans come hammering down against us we were quickly forced to open our eyes and recognise that not all who shared this vast world were content with their lot.

I was young in those days, when it all began. I did not understand the great harm and the terror that awaited us. Our leaders fought amongst themselves. No one could agree. We had after all traded in peace with the people of the great Roman Empire for more moons than any alive could remember.

There were many that believed that the way of Rome was ordained by the Gods and that we ignored their will at our peril, but many feared that Rome would swallow us up and our way of life would be destroyed. Maybe there was a grain of truth in both of these and many of the other reasons given to explain what was happening. But we realised too late that our petty disputes and constant warring amongst ourselves divided our strength and the chance of keeping our world intact. Our conquerers did not care and used this to their own advantage and so during this time of initial confusion the legions of the mighty Roman Empire continued to swoop upon their prey, desecrating all that opposed them and slowly, bit by bit, took control of all.

The ravens of the Dark Mother feasted well as whole tribes and nations made their way to the Hall of our Ancestors. Soon all that remained of our opposition was our Druid stronghold upon the sacred Isle of Anglesey, and so they came and a terrible retribution was paid for our refusal to accept the chains of slavery to Rome. We died upon the Shores of Slaughter, within our groves and all our sacred places were destroyed and to the eyes of Rome we were no more.

But those who stood firm and fought will forever be the true heroes of our heritage, of our blood and we owe them much. This is their story, it is my story and it is your story. Mark it well for there may be a time when this knowledge will stand you in good stead. Ensuring that history does not repeat itself...

A long time ago in a cave, cold, dark and wet
All around us fear and the stench of death
Separate paths our calling made
Knowing we'd never enjoy this life again.

My heart, my soul, we all fought, so brave
Screaming children and our sisterhood we took to our graves
Our life blood spilt and drenched the ground
Amongst the stones and the shore of this sacred land.

So long ago our fate signed, it was so forged
In blood and sacrifice for our sacred course
But still in the woods they whisper our names
With a promise and knowing our time will come again.

So watch the seasons as they change and they turn
And know our time has now returned
Stand strong and gather all your pride
Unveil the inner-self, the wild woman inside.

Oh blessed woman take those hands from your eyes
Then feel the urge surging from deep inside
Buried and suppressed, release those ties
For centuries imprisoned, identity denied

Finally know your worth with your beauty exposed
And shed those shackles and painful chains
Mother and ancient grandmother, warrior and healer too
Knowing dear sisters, you are whoever you choose.

The primal scream, its bonds unleashed
Brings forth the wild woman's release
From enforced captivity, we'll be held no more
Spirit woman, eternal child of our sacred Mother Earth.

Chapter 1
INTO THE BLOOD RED CAVE

The tide has receded leaving the usually submerged rocks glistening in the moonlight. The shell and shingle underfoot is soft, wet and blanketing our feet as we slowly make our way toward the gaping hole. Look to the opening of the cave and know that it is calling and inviting you to sit by the fire at its centre.

The red walls surrounding you dance with shadow and sacred art in the firelight. This is a true place of safety, of sacredness and truth as you are welcomed to your journey within the Blood Red Cave.

So enter the Blood Red Cave, the Nemeton of all women, a place of sanctuary, of teaching, sharing and remembering, a place of celebration, of secrets and memories and of the ancestors, the grandmothers, mothers, daughters, sisters, past, present and future. The Blood Red Cave is within and without. It is the place that we go when we look deep inside ourselves, when we hide, when we need answers and when we need to survive.

It is thought that the Blood Red Cave was the sacred place of women's craft, magic and mysteries. There is a legend that perhaps it became a final place of sanctuary, pain and bloodshed after the Roman massacre of the Druids of Anglesey in 60 CE, though to my knowledge there is little if any historical evidence to support that, apart from the stories of friends who live on Anglesey but just because we have no actual evidence remaining regarding the use of the Anglesey Red Cave, the uses of caves for sacred gatherings and as magical places here in Britain should not be thought of as out of the bounds of possibility.

To have dedicated caves where women (and men) came together and celebrated and practiced their magic and mysteries should be viewed as a natural, realistic and most ancient indigenous practice, one where I believe there is precedence and much evidence pointing to the use of caves in such ways. Places of women's and men's worship, places of the celebration of the sacred feminine and the sacred masculine. These caves, which are thought of as places of spiritual significance, have been discovered in, for example, Altimira, Nerca, Lascaux and Chauvet in Northern Spain and France, dating as far as 30,000 – 40,000 years ago. These stunningly beautiful caves are decorated with paintings, in red ochre and other pigments, of not only animals and hunting scenes but also of the female form and amazing depictions of female genitalia. South African rock art expert David Lewis-Williams suggests that the ancient rock paintings and carvings are best understood as being shamanistic in nature, whilst Le Tuc d'Audoubert maintains that the deeper 'subterranean galleries' should be viewed as having "magical and religious significance". Even here in the United Kingdom, a cave on Gower was discovered in the 1820s containing the remains of an individual who became known as the Red Lady of Paviland. It transpired that the body was that of a young man not a woman and carbon dating estimates him to have died approximately 29,000 years ago. The bones had been painted with red ochre and it was apparent that much care and consideration had been given not only to where the burial took place but how he was buried. He was, we can imagine, buried in a cave of perhaps great significance with apparent ritual and personal consideration with what would seem to be important artefacts which included ivory wands, bracelets and periwinkle shells. We can surmise that these might have been items of his trade and or social standing. So whilst not a red cave specifically, nor a cave that had been decorated with artwork and symbolism, it still gives us a tantalizing window into the importance of the religious significance of caves here in the United Kingdom.

The ritual and spiritual use of caves is also supported by

archaeologist Steve Mithen who puts forward the point that a lot of the depictions are found in very difficult to reach areas within the caves and therefore he contends that these places were only for the privileged few, specific groups or individuals. However, in the caves that focus on the sacred female images of giving birth, of full female forms and of female genitalia, perhaps we can suggest that these are caves dedicated to the Sacred Mother of life and death and of rebirth, Earth Mother caves within the womb of the Great Goddess.

In the last two to three thousand years we have other sources that tell us the cave was a sacred place. Irish and British legends mention them, for example, in Iolo Morgannwg's retailing of 'The Glamorgan Tale' which speaks of the rock fortress beneath the ground known as Craig-y-Dinas and the thousands of sleeping warriors within, or the Arthurian sagas and Merlin's cave of fame, even in the legend of Old Mother Shipton and her magical cave with the fountain of petrifaction and of course the numerous tales of fairy mounds and 'hollow hills'.

A specific example of such a story can be found in the Irish Chronicles, of Conaire the High King and the ritual of choosing him as king. King Eterscel had died and as was the custom a 'bull feast' was arranged to decide who the next king would be. The bull feast was a ritual process that had a very specific function and sections to it. Firstly a bull was chosen and ritually slaughtered, a sacred broth of its flesh would be made and consumed, and its fresh blood drank. Next the freshly flayed hide of the beast was wrapped around the seer. Once this had been done the magical worker retreated to 'sleep', to dream and to prophesy within a sacred place. Through out this process three other priests chanted a continuous magical incantation over the journeying individual until such time as they woke with their vision of who the next king would be

T. W. Rolleston in his book *Celtic Myths and Legends* (1994) quotes Whitley Stokes observations "*So at Aegria, in Achaea, the Priestess of Earth drank the fresh blood of a bull before descending into the cave to prophesy*". The 'Priestesses of Earth' and their use of the cave for divination sounds wonderfully old and hints at a well established tradition that perhaps might have involved other rituals that can no longer be guessed at. T.W.Rolleston suggests that the rituals and magical practice attributed to the Celtic people and their priests the Druids can be thought of as actually belonging to a much earlier indigenous people. He points out that Druidism and Celtic spirituality only exists where the Celtic population migrated to lands of the Dolmen builders of Western Europe. Here he contends that they (the Celts) found *"people with a powerful priesthood, a ritual and imposing religious monuments; a people steeped in magic and mysticism and a cult of the Underworld. The inferences, as I read the facts, seem to be that druidism in its essential features was imposed upon the imaginative and sensitive nature of the Celts....The Celt with his extraordinary aptitude for 'picking up ideas' by the earlier population, the Megalithic People of Western Europe".* I agree with this viewpoint and I believe that it supports my own personal belief that caves did hold important significance to our prehistoric ancestors, and continued to do so for thousands of years in one form or another, thus becoming part of our unconscious fabric of being, woven into the very DNA of who we are.

There is a place on Anglesey that might just hold the key. Only half a mile off the main bridge that crosses the Meni Straights is Llanfairpwllgwyngyllogerychwyrndrobwllllanfyliogogogoch. The name of the village that holds this famous and extremely long name is translated as 'St Mary's Church in the hollow of the white hazel near the whirlpool of St Tysilio by the Red Caves.' So Gogogoch actually means the 'Red Caves' and is usually the only part of this village's name that anyone, including me, can remember and pronounce. I also understand that it is in this village that one of the earliest Women's Institutes was founded; women's magic appears to not have left this amazing and sacred place.

Sadly the hazel has long gone but the church remains and was built by the side of the tree because it was an important Pagan shrine. It is believed that offerings were left inside it up until it no longer remained a recognised sacred place but even though this site's origins may have been forgotten as a place of pagan worship, I would suggest that actually the threads that defined its spiritual significance never diminished and have indeed prevailed even if it is only the site of a very old church, which still remains to this day. Perhaps it is not unthinkable to suggest that the hazel was the marker to the caves that were below.

At one time you could get to the caves by passing through the churchyard and down onto the beach via a cliff path, which would have been pretty precarious as this had to be judged between the high and low tides when the caves were visible. This path can no longer be followed and the caves are inaccessible as the sea has risen significantly over the last two thousand years and they are now permanently under water. The cave does exist and is known by the name I have given and though access is denied by the tides of the Irish Sea, its magic is intact and its mysteries are protected, with its walls red and forever wet, making it truly a place between the worlds.

The cave is a place I have known all of my life in some capacity or another, whether in the recurring and terrifying dreams that I had from childhood until recent years, to the knowledge, strength and courage that I have drawn from it in my adult life.

Travelling into the Blood Red Cave is a journey into who and what we are, accessing that secret and most sacred of places where we seek sanctuary within. It is here that we store our most precious things - our hopes, dreams and even our fears. Within the cave we forge the armour that we wear to face the challenges that life throws at us. It is the place where we warm ourselves at the eternal fire that burns, where we drink from the overflowing horn that bestows courage, strength and determination, where we nourish ourselves so that we might flourish, where we find personal empowerment. The Blood Red Cave is the womb from which we give birth and where we, in turn, are birthed. It honours all the phases of womanhood with the ritual, magic and mystery that make us who we are. It is our connection with the ancestral grandmothers whose essence we still carry, who will always walk by our sides. It is a gateway, a doorway to Annwn.

Here is our temple of the Great Goddess which we empower with ritual that calls upon all that we are, with all elemental forces joined, the land, sea, sky and wind forging, shaping and honing us. Understand this as a place of awesome power, for in this place we are complete and we are whole. It becomes the source and the elixir that feeds and nourishes us and the labyrinth that is our personal journey through life.

As a child I had a recurring nightmare and I would wake crying and shaking with terror. My mother would always comfort me and tell me it was just a dream, but this dream was different and it never left me even as an adult. The dream was always the same: I was in a cave full of women and children. Some of us were wearing black and carrying weapons. Many of us were injured and some even dying. There was blood everywhere and the echoes of crying, pain and death were all around me. Older women dressed in black robes and funny black hats that had twirly little points, rather like pigtails, leaned against the cave walls wailing and calling out in a language I didn't understand and yet I somehow recognised. I was pacing backwards and forward over the uneven ground and I was covered in blood, particularly down my right side and all over the arm that held a small short sword. The smell of the sea had mingled with the sweat, blood and fear that covered me. There was so much grief it was overwhelming.

My feelings were of extreme loss and despair. If I was injured I didn't notice but I was angry and frustrated. As I looked to the mouth of the cave there was a man pacing up and down. I knew this man and yet I also knew that soon he would be dead, along with anyone else who was found within the cave. It was a feeling of total devastation and despair, and it is always at this point I wake up. I should mention that even as a very young child having this dream I was not a child in the cave, I was a young woman.

It was many, many years before I had any insight into this dream and any true understanding of its significance. Of course, there is now a lot more to tell regarding this particular dream and of the journey that I have taken as a result. However, that is for another time and maybe another book. One thing I can say is this, as far as I am concerned, my recurring dream was my first journey into the Blood Red Cave, a past life memory or an ancestral memory, it matters not because I have always known that it was part of me; it is a connection so tangible and so very real, and that is what was important.

As I said earlier the cave can be accessed in different ways and will be whatever is relevant and needed at that point in time. Within this book I am sharing some of my experiences and magical journeys that have taken me into the Blood Red Cave. However, the following took place not too long ago and documents the first of several journeys that I made over the space of a few weeks.

At my cabin in Swithland Woods, I had prepared myself. The wood stove was doing its job and the place felt snug and warm, candles were lit whilst under foot the sheepskins and cushions covered the floor in readiness to begin. The light was fading fast from outside and a quiet stillness now hung in the air. Finally I lit the charcoal and once it glowed white I covered it with incense that I had made especially for the occasion.

My sacred space was ready and I was ready. I sat cross-legged in the middle of the room and picked up my journey drum that I had placed to one side in readiness; and so it began a slow rhythmic beat, softly at first, but just loud enough to feel the vibration through my body. As I called out to the spirits of place, to my ancestors and to the guardians of the three realms, my drumming grew louder. I stated my intent loud and clear, I requested entrance to the world of my ancestors and to meet with my most ancient of grandmothers. I called to them saying that I sought their wisdom that I might be shown that which is relevant and needed. I asked to be guided and let it be known that I felt no fear and that there was nothing to fear from me, that I would be protected at all times, and so it went as I called to the Blood Red Cave.

The drumming stopped and I closed my eyes. The image that came was the pathway that I usually walk into woods where my cabin is situated.

I followed the path quite contently, looking about me to see what I could see and sense. The woods had a different feel, a soft iridescent glow, an awakeness and crispness that somehow, regardless of its beauty is hidden on my non magical journeys into it.

I turned now to my left and up through the bracken that was already retreating back to the earth in readiness for the approaching winter. I walked up a slight hill, until I reached the top where a clearing opened up. I knew where I was of course, the Oak Grove. The sky was clear and I could see the stars shining through the high branches. I could hear an owl not too far away calling into the night and the scrabbling of the woodland creatures in the undergrowth.

I stood for a while not sure what to do next and just as I felt that perhaps I should call out, I felt a low rumble beneath my feet that progressively got louder as the shaking earth pulled apart in front of my eyes. The centre of the grove split open like a ripe fruit before me and the force threw me to the ground. As I looked up the roots of an enormous oak filled the gaping hole that would have been in the ground. By this time I was standing again and all was calm again in the grove.

As I walked toward the upturned tree I saw the start of a staircase that corkscrewed downward into darkness and into the belly of the Earth Mother. Then without thinking, because I just knew that this was the door and also the invitation, climbing on to the staircase, I began my decent. Down and down I stepped, the branches of the tree stretching out to the sides of me providing added protection and preventing me from falling.

It is strange to be climbing down an upturned tree knowing that as you step each step towards the ground, you are also stepping higher into the canopy of the tree. When eventually I did step off of the last stair and on to the ground, I did not see the person who was there waiting and yet I was aware that whoever it was, that the person was male.

The ground was covered in crisp white snow and it was very cold and I remember thinking that as usual I was so appropriately dressed for the occasion and conditions -not! I have been known in my time, to climb mountains in floaty silks and velvets (all I can say is it felt like a good idea at the time). However, in fairness and in my own defence with regards to this particular instance, I had no idea I would be taken to a place of ice and snow.

On both sides stood beautifully tall pine trees partially blanketed with snow and with crystal clear icicles hanging from their branches. It was from behind one of these trees that my guide stepped. He was not particularly tall and I could not really make out his face as he was covered head to foot in furs and skins tied on with leather thongs. I could see that he had a very dark beard that protruded from under his hood and for the brief time that he initially looked at me, I could see that his eyes were dark. He did not speak at all but walked off down the trackway between the pine trees and I had the overwhelming feeling that I was expected to follow, so I did.

A little way in front of us I could just make out the mouth of a cave set into the rock face. However as we approached I could then see the two large decorated and painted stones that stood either side of the entrance to the cave. Stunning and spectacular are words I would use, the reds and greens and blues standing out against the greyish stone and the brilliant white of the snow, but words somehow seem inadequate. The entrance to the cave itself was also painted and decorated with the most elaborate spirals and labyrinth designs.

Inside, the cave itself was big, airy and surprisingly light. The floor was smooth and hard and a welcoming fire was lit in a central circular fire pit radiating warmth and comfort. Skins were hung upon the walls along with painted images of women dancing, giving birth and participating in other activities that I couldn't quite make out. The whole thing was an amazing spectacle, but more importantly, I felt that this was a sacred and ancient place and that without doubt this place was protected and therefore so was I.

I had not noticed my guide for some time but suddenly he seemed to appear out of nowhere from deep within the shadow at the back of the cave. He beckoned me to follow him again, which of course I did. Completely hidden to me beforehand I now saw the narrow passage and the well worn steps cut into the stone that took me deeper into the cave. It was here that my guide left me, his last instructions were to point me in the direction I need to walk, and so I was alone again.

Out of the darkness I heard water and as I followed the narrow passage of steps around and down, where again my breath was taken away, the steps finally gave way and everything opened up into the most vast of chasms. It was so big, There appeared to be hundreds of lit torches hanging from the walls giving the place a slight pungent smell and a low lying veil of smoky mist, so adding to the magical and mystical atmosphere of this other worldly place. This was truly a beautiful place with an underground river flowing through its centre and stalactites and stalagmites everywhere. I could see large stone boulders that formed a bridge across the river so I made my way down to cross to the other side.

It was as I approached the water that I saw a large log-like vessel move away from the opposite bank. The vessel had been made from what looked like a hollowed tree trunk; it still had the bark on the outer sides. As I got closer I realised that this tree boat was not empty and that within it lay a woman, or should I say I knew that she was dead, there was certainly no movement from her and she had the complexion of powdered chalk. There was a beauty and nobility about this woman and her final journey. She was covered in a patchwork of furs and a blanket of fresh pine branches, her dark hair woven with twigs and leaves and leather cord and she wore bone beads about her neck and what looked like a slight smile upon her face. A painted drum lay at her feet and a highly carved wooden staff on her right side and an old leather pouch on her left. She took with her her most prized possessions and those that would be of use to her on her journey and thereafter.

This was a peaceful and dignified scene that was surrounded by a strange stillness as she floated past me, taken by the river into the darkness ahead and out of my sight. I remember feeling the warm tears fall from my eyes and wondering why there had been nobody else but me at this lady's passing and I called to the Goddess and spirits of place to welcome this woman and keep her safe.

After a while I continued my journey but my mind was still on the events that I had just witnessed as I proceeded to cross the river. It was here that the three women were waiting as I jumped off of the last boulder. Two seemed to be fairly young whilst the third woman, who stood in-between the younger ones, was beautiful with her slightly weatherworn face and white hair. I would imagine that she was not as old as I thought her to be; nonetheless, she had the air of wisdom and of being somebody who was used to being listened to and when the need arose, obeyed. There was such warmth and a sense of belonging that again I was more than happy to follow these women. Nothing was said to me however. The younger women chatted quietly between themselves and every so often looked back at me and smiled. Strange as it sounds, I really felt that not only were they expecting me but that they were also pleased to see me, which all added to the vague familiarity about everything that I had.

Having crossed the river I noticed how different it felt and so much brighter, due in part to the massive torches resting in stone brackets carved into the walls. I was taken a little way from the river to a sort of alcove. There were several women at work in various areas with herbs, water and fire; they all in turn looked up and acknowledged me with a smile and then continued with what they had been doing.

Skins, heathers and fresh greenery covered the floor giving off a gentle musky and aromatic smell as I walked upon it. Along the back of the wall in the alcove, a bed like large shelf had been cut and then covered in furs and heather. Upon the shelf lay a naked woman in the throws of giving birth. She made very little noise but by now all the women had gathered close and were singing a low and vibrating song as they gently swayed in rhythm helping the birthing woman with their spell of intent. It was so moving and beautifully haunting, it was so right and everything about it felt absolutely natural and as it should be.

As I moved closer, I realised the entire wall along this birthing shelf was covered in hundreds of handprints of blood, made by each of the women from their birthing blood after their babies had come into the world. How did I know this? I don't know, I just did and it was an amazing sight.

The air smelt of burning pine needles that had been placed on the roaring fire that was slightly elevated on a stone platform and it was here that the older woman moved toward me. From beneath the stone platform she lifted a gorgeous patchwork fur cloak and placed it about my shoulders. From the large pouch hanging from her waist she produced a smaller pouch and gave this to me. Within this gift I found a small bone needle and sinew thread, a small amount of dried herbs, a very sharp flint and what I thought was a bone talisman of some kind. It had a flat round top and the body formed a bit like a long teardrop but it was covered in carved ridges all the way down. Just as I thought she had finished she beckoned one of the younger women forward and presented me with my own yew staff. I was shocked at this and very surprised and a little confused, I don't mind admitting. The young woman just smiled gave me a quick hug. I thanked both women for their kindness and gifts and apologised that I had brought nothing to give them; I hoped that they understood as still nobody had spoken to me.

The older woman stepped forward and took my arm and slowly guided me back to the river and the bridge. I understood that it was time to go and so I thanked her again. In return she bent over and picked up a handful of the damp earth from the water's edge, and she proceeded to mark me on both cheeks and my forehead. It was then clear that I should cross the bridge and so I did, strangely feeling sadness and if I am honest, knowing that I did not want to go. I looked back once I reached the other side but she was gone. In fact, to my surprise, everything was in darkness and I could see nothing.

I was about to retrace my steps back to the upper cave when I noticed an altar to my right I had not seen this on my arrival. It was cut out of and carved into a huge rock that rested against the cave wall. There was again a small fire burning on top of it and holes that had been carved in front of and all around the fire. There I saw hundreds of tiny umbilical cords that had been left as offerings within and around the carved holes. I decided to make my own offering and so I cut a piece of my sinew thread with the flint and placed that in one of the holes with some of the dried herbs I had been given. I noticed that other offerings had also been made of small bones and stone tools and beads. Again I felt overwhelmed for some reason that I couldn't quite explain to myself. All I can say is that I know it was the right thing to do.

My offering made I then quickly made my way back to the narrow passage of steps and back up into the entrance cave. Everything was as I had left it, warm and welcoming but the cave opening seemed larger and drawing me towards it. As I stepped out of the doorway and onto the snow the cold bit at me and I saw my guide again waiting patiently as he leaned against one of the great stone pillars. As soon as he saw me he set off down the track toward the upturned oak and I followed, reluctantly I will admit but knowing that my time here was at an end, at least for the time being. At the bottom (or top of the tree, depending on how you look at it) my guide surprised me by suddenly grabbing my left arm, wrapping a leather cord around the top of it. Beads dangled from the ends that were bone and delicately carved. I thanked him and turned to start my climb of this enormous tree and back to the oak grove. I looked back once as I stepped onto the staircase and just as before he was gone and everything was in darkness and I could see nothing.

I will not bore you with the following bit of my journey. Nothing out of the ordinary took place and it wasn't too long before I reached the oak grove. After following the path back and out of the woods, I opened my eyes and found myself back in my cabin, in the dark and shivering because the wood stove had long gone out and all of my candles had burnt down and I felt starving hungry.

This was the first of several journeys to my Blood Red Cave and throughout the rest of this book I will share other journeys that I have made which have all proven to be significant with a profound effect and impact on my life.

JOURNEYING INTO THE BLOOD RED CAVES

The Blood Red Caves are real and not an abstract concept, but they are also what I shall refer to as 'liminal'. Liminal literally means 'a threshold', and I shall use the term in this book to indicate being 'between the worlds', the boundaries that you step over into other states of consciousnesses and realities. These states of being (and places) are not easy to define and can be subjective. However, the liminal world is the experience of journeying outside of what we know and what we normally perceive. Therefore we can step over the threshold into other realities of limitless possibilities. In this place of liminality we are walking between the worlds and so our personal caves will also exists by definition, because it has reality and meaning to us. When we journey within the caves they represent us, our lives, our experiences and the ancestry of who we are. They are a treasure trove to be explored and found and to be used, thus creating a bridge that can span the generations.

So let us paint a picture in our mind's eye that will take us deep inside ourselves providing an internal road map to who and what we are. Think of the Cave as a doorway to an endless labyrinth of other caves, each with its own purpose, its own hidden mysteries and its secrets to share, each with knowledge of a time and a place and each stretching back to the beginning of all things.

Below I have written Part 1 of the initial journey you might want to follow to reach the caves. It might be helpful if you have somebody read this part of the journey for you, or maybe you can record yourself reading it so that you can play it back and use it whenever you need to. Either way it should be whatever is easiest and preferable for you.

You will notice that in each of the chapters there is a meditation journey into a different cave, Please always start by referring back to Part 1 of the journey as written here in this chapter, Part 2 of your journey 'The Cave' will be yours. I will put in some suggestions for you to follow and that are relevant depending on the cave you are visiting, but on the whole this is about your experience, what you see, what you learn, and what you take from the experience. Part 3 of your journey, The Return, should always be followed for any of the meditation journeys that you take.

Part 1: The Journey
Make yourself comfortable, you may want to lie down, you may feel happy sitting, it really is about what you feel is best for you. Make sure you are warm, switch the phone off and close the curtains if it is too bright for you. This is your journey of self discovery into the magic and wisdom held within the Blood Red Caves.

Close your eyes, or perhaps you might feel you aren't quite ready yet, either way it doesn't really matter, you are comfortable and beginning to feel the waves of relaxation ripple slowly down through the whole of your body. Focus on the rise and fall of your chest, of every breath in and every slow breath out, allowing you to relax releasing any stress and tension that you may have….it's easy…..easy as breathing….breathing in and breathing out.

Maybe you are still aware of surrounding noises, of outside traffic, of music playing in the distance or of my voice drifting in and out of your mind…but that's ok, your mind is becoming just a little more aware as your consciousness begins to shift and move, shifting and moving and opening the doors to other realms and opening doors to other parts of yourself and to an altered state of awareness.

But for the moment you are just beginning this journey and nothing matters. Accept your feelings of deepening relaxation, of being stress free and of being comfortable. Now perhaps your eyes are beginning to get just a little heavy, perhaps they are so heavy they now want to close, or perhaps they are already closed, closed and allowing you to relax a little further. Your eyes might now be feeling so heavy they just don't want to open, but that's all right, you don't mind because you know that you are so relaxed, that your eyes have relaxed, letting the feeling wash over and through the entirety of your body.

So in a moment I will ask you to take a deep breath in...ok... so take a breath in long and deep holding if for a moment of time and then as you exhale out... feel the tensions of the day leave your body as you begin to truly relax. Feel yourself float deeper and deeper as the air leaves your lungs...deeper and deeper, but more and more relaxed as you now breathe normally and steadily again...now in your own time.... breathe in deeply again and hold for another moment of time...that's right...just feel the air as it fills your lungs...and then as you breathe out feel yourself floating down and down and down... deeper and deeper, letting go of all the stresses and tensions of your life, letting go of any troubles that might usually occupy your mind... just let go and feel the total warmth of the ripples of relaxation flowing freely through every part of your body.... relaxing each and every part from the top of your head to the tip of your toes...feel the exquisite relaxation as every part of you lets go...that's right...everything just letting go, letting go, releasing and relaxing.

Now as you continue to relax you hear a beat, it is the beat of your heart, a beat that is steady and reassuring, hear it getting louder and know it as being forever constant, know it as your anchor and your personal ancestral rhythm.... your own personal rhythm that enables you to dance through life ...a sacred rhythm that holds the secrets and mysteries of life...your life...of past lives of those in your line from long ago...listen...listen as it takes you on this journey... listen as your internal drum beats... oh so gently..... but oh so strongly....

a beat that is familiar and comforting that takes you deeper still..... deeper and deeper into the place you need to go......down and down and down...into the other realms of self...drifting down and down to the Blood Red Caves, feeling totally relaxed, totally safe and free of all other worldly anxieties and concerns, leaving you free to explore, free to discover and free to experience.

In a moment you are going to feel the ground beneath your feet as you land softly onto the path leading you to the opening of the caves which you can see a little way off. Look around you as you find your feet again, still feeling relaxed and feeling confident and ready to explore.

Where are your caves set? Are they carved into the hillside, a grand ancestral chamber with other chambers leading off in various directions creating a labyrinth of stone, moss and green? Or are your caves set into the side of the cliffs somewhere? Is the path leading to them pebble and sand, with large rocks standing to attention either side of the cave opening? Is the sea wild and full of life as its waves break over the surrounding beach? Where are you? But maybe, just maybe your caves are somewhere completely different, but you are not worried because it matters not......these are your caves and they will be wherever you are and where ever you need them to be...

Look around you as you now walk to the cave.....beautiful and vibrant colours mingle sky, fauna and flora together....there is an exaggerated natural beauty in this world, an energy that feeds and revitalizes you.....it is a truly wonderful feeling that will not leave you even when you leave this place because you know it is an essential part of who you are. Each step closer to the cave gives you a feeling of empowerment of strength and focus... you are the sum total of all who have been before you, you are the present and you are the expectation of what is still to come....this is a special and sacred place to be, a place of self nurturing, self renewal and personal wisdom.... And as you finely reach the opening to your cave you feel the power radiating from within, radiating and knowing it is holding you, protecting you

….you feel it now as it joins with you, sharing with you and guiding you as you now take your first steps into the Blood Red Caves.

Part 2: Into the Caves

You are now in the first chamber of the caves. This is the welcoming chamber, it can be whatever you need it to be but know it as safe and protecting and a place to relax and perhaps just sit allowing yourself to lose yourself in the moment.

Once you have entered, warm yourself by the hearth fire and look around you. What memories, stones and treasures have you put away on the shelves of the red walls that are glistening and dripping with water? What secret dreams and aspirations did you put down and push to the back of the cave? What ambitions, inspiration and creativity can you see covered in cobwebs and dust, quiet and untended in your mind's eye, lest they should ignite again a longing, of unfulfilled childhood emotions, of believing that you are invincible and that anything is possible?

Everywhere you look within the cave has meaning, just as everything within the caves is part of you, part of the past, part of the present and part of what is yet to be.

Part 3: The Return and Awakening

(This should be recorded then played back or read out to enable you to return and awaken from your journey.)

When you are ready and you are happy that it is time to leave, make your way back out of the cave and onto the pathway. However this time when you are on the path you see a large rock a little way in front of you and as you walk toward it you see a large door within the rock face.

Now I want you to listen again to me, in a moment I am going to count from ten down to one and as I count down you will begin to return to this time and this place, and once you hear the number one called you will be able to open your eyes. You will be fully awake, refreshed, relaxed and will remember all that has transpired on your journey.

Now when you are ready open the door and step through closing the door behind you. As you turn back you now see a flight of stairs going up in front of you, with ten steps in total.

Ten, you begin to climb, *nine, eight, seven,* you are now becoming more aware of your surroundings as you continue to climb back to this time and place. *Six, five, four,* you are becoming more and more awake, *three, two*, almost there and now your eyes are ready to open. *One*, your eyes open and you have returned, relaxed, refreshed, energised and empowered.

Gently allow yourself to re-acclimatise into your body and the room that you are in and in due course take a deep breath and exhale, have a really good stretch and a good all over shake to make sure you are totally back in your body and everything is awake and happy.

It is important to make sure to have something to eat and drink, perhaps a biscuit and a glass of water. This helps to ground you and re-anchor you in this time and space. If you can, keep a diary of your experiences and know that the cave is there whenever and if ever you need it, and will never leave you.

Chapter 2
THE CAVE OF THE DANCING MAIDEN

The Maiden of Spring, the Muse of Inspiration
Sacred moon and maidens true
In boughs of green and moon-blood new
Spring forth and circle morning's first dew
Then circle the milk of the mother ewe
Your third a circle of acorns true
In faith of life from the Mother's womb.

The Song of the Maiden

As the gaping hole between the Goddess's legs opens, the dark is momentarily lit from without. From the depths within the bulging woman the last throws of pain, of torn skin and excrement as the spasm-ridden body in rhythm with itself is in raptures as new life springs forth from her. The ultimate in sacrifice has been made.

The gaping hole closes enough so that the illusion of silence and dark returns. Welcome the Maiden, the waxing moon, the child of inspiration and all that's new.

The land slowly lifts her head and shakes herself awake. The sap of new leaves stirs upon the branches. The shoots from the warmth of the Mother make their way into the light. The breath of air is warmer and the cold of winter is blown gently to one side. The promise of all that is to come hangs like crystals and precious gems, each one unique in its own potential, each one without compromise, each one without limitations.

The cloak of youth wraps tightly around the Maiden, her beauty without question: she is the muse, the inspiration, the dream, the creativity. She is unstoppable. Washed clean and nourished by the rains, her growth is in shades of greens, yellows and blues, for she is the goddess of fire, born of the earth, cradled in air and fed by the running waters. She is elemental energy newly forged but of an eternal source that is timeless in its cycle of regeneration and its commitment to re-birth and life.

Know her as the child who is not afraid, the child whose dreams reach for the skies, understand her for the innocence she radiates, for daring to be individual and independent. No mountain is too high for her to climb with her aspirations full of the truest magic: self belief, self worth and unlimited potential.

She does not understand compromise and is selfish in her needs. Petulant and temperamental if told "no" too often, ferocious in her battle to strike out in the world and make her mark, to be noticed, loved and adored. But for all her perceived youth she harbours ancestral knowledge that is within her very being, that is clear in its message and that supports her through to the end. She is survival through truth and the understanding of the blessing that is "I". I am she as she is me. This chain cannot be broken for we are one and the same in this never-ending cycle. Like the tree as it sings the song of tree, so the Maiden is only interested in singing the song of the Maiden. It is but for the briefest of times, as she knows that all things must pass and yet when she is forgotten or unseen, her truth is that she still remains at the heart of everything and every being.

The Virgin

Over the last few thousand years, mistranslations and maybe a desire to control and disempower women has viewed the Maiden as a pure and virginal character. Christian and patriarchal societies have used this as a means to debase the sacred feminine, lowering the maiden to a weak, fragile individual in need of male protection and ultimately the chattel and property of her father and any man to whom he has seen fit to give her. But the Maiden as the uninitiated, naive in the ways of the world, emotional, pure, untouched before marriage is a false and misleading lie. The true translation of 'virgin' is as a daughter and priestess of Ver, goddess of fire and water, an aspect of the Great Mother Goddess Ur. She is an independent woman in her own right and therefore she belongs to no one but herself.

Imbolc

There are many ways to welcome the Maiden, to honour the fiery passion and desire for life anew. Imbolc is the first festival and celebration associated with the great maiden goddess Brid. The Winter Solstice now behind us and the darkness beginning to lift, the sun gently starts its journey and ascent. The warmth is close at hand and the nights not so long and the days not quite so short.

All through the dark months the Yule log is kept alight to remind us that the light and the warmth of the sun and of the summer will return. On the eve of Imbolc (1st Feb), the Yule fires within the home are dowsed, but a log or ember from the Yule fire is taken just before, and it is from this that the great fire of Imbolc is lit. The women of the house or tribe carry out this sacred task, guarding and maintaining a vigil until the rising of the sun marking Imbolc.

Throughout their vigil the women feast together, they sing and dance and tell stories around the fire. They honour the Maiden as she promises them life anew. All their dreams, aspirations, plans and hopes are called out, the seeds have been sown and the excitement that any pregnant mother may feel as she labours is given voice, for this is the birth of the Maiden and a time to rejoice, having survived through the dark time. The first stirrings of life can be seen and felt, the first signs that the wheel has once again turned.

Within ourselves we honour the child, the joy of innocence and all that has to offer. It is a time of growth, creativity and inspiration and as the Maiden grows so do we. Our bodies change, our breasts begin to form, the hair and smell of puberty can be seen and experienced because just as nature around us matures, so do we. The maiden begins her first true sacrifice, the flux or moon blood, which signifies that the maiden is fully grown; just as she sacrifices her own life source, she now has the potential to give life. Traditionally a time of celebration, the first blood should be honoured. This is truly women's magic and an acknowledgement of life. The first moon-blood is collected and given back to the Great Mother Earth; the women gather to welcome the young maiden to the sisterhood and her first rite of passage has begun.

The cycle for the Maiden has come full circle and soon she will enter the house of the Mother. Our ancestors understood this power more than we do today; they came together and bled together and this was a time of teaching, the sharing of song and dance and resting, women honouring women, handing down women's magic and craft, celebrating the Goddess within, engaging in personal as well as communal ritual. This was not a place or time but women in their power, governed by the Moon Goddess, nurtured and protected by the Great Mother Goddess.

It is the 1st of February and the sky is a beautiful clear blue, although the wind is harsh and cold, whipping at people as they go about their daily business, everyone hurrying and wondering if the promised snow will indeed fall and interfere with their already hectic lives. But tonight I, along with friends, will enter the ancient woods of Swithland in Leicestershire and we will awaken the Serpent of the Land. We will honour the Maiden in all her guises, we will call to the Goddess of Fire, born of the earth, cradled in air and nourished by the running waters to awaken and bring back life anew to the sleeping land. We will have re-ignited the Cave of the Dancing Maiden that represents the spring in all things.

Imbolc, the festival of lactating ewes, heralds the return of the Maiden Goddess in all her glory. We are inspired to shake off the cloak of winter and embrace the return of the light and warmth of the

Sun God. And just as the priestesses before me, I too will awaken Gogyerwin, Serpent Goddess of the land, with the eternal chant "*I will not harm the serpent and the serpent will not harm me*". I don't remember where I got this chant from, but I understand it to have been the call of priestesses from over two thousand years ago at Imbolc. Regardless of whether or not it has the validity of an authentic chant calling to us from antiquity, it still has relevance and the intent still rings true.

Life Experience

I have been reminded lately of so many things from my past and in particular from my childhood that are important to who and what I am, and yet so much until recently I had forgotten or filed into the dark recesses of my mind. The Maiden aspect done and dusted, forgotten and yet still such a vital part of me - how easily we forget as life and the mundane gets in the way.

So as this is the time of re-birth and a time of reconnection please indulge me as I lift the rusty lid that has remained closed for so long and share some of my own story with you, thus reconnecting and re-igniting the Maiden within me and hopefully you.

I didn't take part in the grown ups' rituals as a young child but I, like all children, embraced the true essence of the Maiden. I ran free amongst the old oak and elm trees that lived next to our house, the remains of the old Kingswood forest in South Gloucestershire. I was a child of nature, barefoot most of the time, hair tangled and unruly, wilful and full of the joys of spring. I was adoring of my friend the old oak who stood so tall and proud at the bottom of road and just outside our garden, his spirit so kind and wise and so protecting. I played for hours beneath him, singing him my songs and telling him stories and listening to him as he shared his secrets in return. He taught me to be still and observe; he showed me the magic of living and the beauty around me. He took care of all the creatures that lived within his branches, never complaining but always generous, wise from his hundreds of years upon this earth. A true inspiration and a wonderment to a young child who believed herself every bit as magical creature as those she saw about her.

No one at that point had ever told her that magic didn't exist or that what she saw was nothing more than an overactive imagination. She had no concept that the majority of society had lost their connection with the natural magic of nature and of the sacred landscape and along with all things considered fairy tale and make believe and therefore feared and dismissed this part of themselves. As I was told many years later 'there is no scientific proof that any magical reality exists and people who claim to see, live and practice this way of life are charlatans preying on the vulnerabilities of others'. In other words I didn't and wouldn't conform to the accepted social norms, and I wouldn't be brainwashed and or controlled by the accepted powers that be. I have to thank the Gods for that, and as I have said before what an unbelievably boring world it would be if we all did!

I was brought up on the stories of the elementals, of the Fair Folk, of the magic that resides within all of us and the spirit and the stories of the land. I was taught to understand the Wheel of the Year and the importance of that cycle and my place within it. My grandpy always called it the 'the way of the country folk'. It did not occur to me until I was much older that this was not the norm, that most adults and children around me did not share the same beliefs or take any notice of the magical worlds. As I grew older I scared many of my friends and yet at the same time was a constant curiosity.

However, from about the age of four or five I suppose my most precious possession was my little grey case. It doubled as my altar, although let's be honest I didn't really understand it as being that at the time, but that in truth is what it was. My little grey case was full of all my most precious things, stones and pebbles that I had found, or I had been given, but they all had special meaning and onto each one I had painted magical and secret symbols of which, only I and the Fair Folk knew the meanings. My case also contained sprigs of lavender and rosemary, plaited grass and flower circlets which I often used to leave as offerings to the fairy folk and to the spirit of the trees, particularly my friend the old oak. I had several very small china animals; one or two of them came from Christmas crackers, the cow and the robin which sat on a log, and a pig that came from a gift shop in Torquay. I absolutely believed that all of them were extremely magical and had great powers.

The other contents of my case consisted of twigs and acorns, feathers and a hanky with a lace trim with my initial embroidered in the corner which was given to me by Nanny Watson, and a perfume bottle, one of my mum's old Avon bottles I believe, that I would fill with water and flower petals, and this I used to anoint myself and my little china animals. And of course there was the little clay bowl that I had made. The bottom of the case was always covered with dried flowers that I had picked at some time or another, the remains of daisy chains, evening primrose and dried leaves from the trees. I can still remember the smell when I opened it, a warm comforting smell of earth and greens, lavender and rosemary, with faint hints of rose and wild flowers.

Wherever I went so did my little grey case. When it was open I would lay out the hanky and place all of my sacred and precious belongings upon it and always put cake or biscuit crumbs into the bowl as an offering, Interesting I should remember the crumbs; the likelihood is that was all there was left after I had eaten the rest. Nevertheless, when it was time to pack things away the crumbs would be placed at the bottom of my oak tree or given back to the earth by placing the contents of the bowl under a bush or just on the grass along with the last remains of any drink I had with me. As children we often went out for the whole day and mum would make us a picnic to take, even if we were only the other side of the garden wall. We were always on an adventure and always that adventure was to a magical realm and even magical beings get hungry!

We played so openly with the elemental spirits, building

elaborate houses of grass, adorning ourselves and everything around us with wildflower garlands. There was an abundance of evening primrose, wild poppies, daisies, dandelions and occasionally any other flower we could nick from the surrounding gardens. If it was late summer we would have bowls of blackberries we had picked and even loganberries if we were at our aunt's. We danced and sang and held our magic for all the other children to join in. I don't remember ever being unhappy or sad during those times and even then we truly walked between the worlds.

The time of the Dancing Maiden is the realisation and the practical application of rituals and rites of passage that focus on and honour the spirit and inspiration of youth. This process provides an opportunity for us to openly accept and face the difficult transitions in our lives, in this case, from childhood to adulthood or from winter to spring and all that that brings. It is a form of rebirth, of moving on and therefore can have powerful and emotive implications for us as individuals and on those around us.

RITES OF PASSAGE - MAIDEN

This time is an acknowledgement of achievement and of gaining of respect within your peer group, family, tribe and community. My experience both as an individual and as a mother has shown me that as a young person although you might recognise and understand the importance of what you are participating in, it is not until you get older, and perhaps have children of your own, that the true meaning, the value and the preciousness of the whole experience becomes apparent. But nothing is gained without sacrifice and so I believe there should always be some aspect of personal challenge and a facing of fears within any ritual or rite of passage. It represents reality and therefore is a true reflection of life and of living. Life can be hard sometimes. Over and over again through different experiences and events in our lives we are challenged, emotionally, physically or on any other level. Facing challenges and your fears within ritual acknowledges this fact.

It shows you that you can face the darkness and overcome hardships. It highlights an inner strength that will stand you in good stead throughout your life, enabling you to face whatever life throws at you. It reinforces that in life you rarely get something for nothing and within craft we understand this as meaning nothing is gained without sacrifice.

In the case of the maiden, she is leaving her childhood behind her and in doing so faces the reality of personal responsibility. This is a very difficult concept for adults, let alone for a young person. It has been my experience that it is just as difficult for any parent to relinquish some of their parental control and responsibilities and allow the young person to take this step whilst honouring what is sure to transpire in the days, months and years ahead.

My daughter's rite of passage was a difficult one for a lot of different reasons. Traditionally you would expect to celebrate a young girl's coming of age when she starts her monthly bleed. However, my daughter decided she wanted to wait until she was eighteen, which on reflection was the right thing for her and is in keeping with current society's ideas regarding the coming of age and acknowledgement of young people reaching adulthood.

My daughter's rite of passage was a personal affair, with only a few selected women who had been influential in her upbringing along with a few chosen friends. In preparation during Beltane, I gathered a sizeable sprig from the broom bush that resides in the garden of my cabin in Swithland Woods. I made sure I chose a part of the plant that had a long stem. The rod was bushy on the end and in full bloom, displaying brightly coloured yellow flowers. This I hung to dry until it would be needed later in the year. It is my understanding that the 'bushrod' is the true witch's broom, rather than the broom of popular mythology which in my family is known as a besom and is, not surprisingly, only used for sweeping floors or garden paths and not, unfortunately, for flying around on under a full moon.

The bushrod is the tool of protection, of cleansing, and can be used in the preparation of sacred space. It can be used in the same way as a traditional wand for setting up and casting circles if that is your preferred way. I have also used it to awaken, by banging the rod end three times on the floor or on my altar, the spirits of place or the elemental energies and entities that I wish to work with. It is used in much the same way, in this case, as a staff might be. However, the bushrod means more than this within my family as it is my grandmother's family name and so has ancestral relevance as well as its spiritual use and magical application.

I was once in a quaint little teashop in Dorset, (eating cinnamon buns, as you do), where displayed on the wall was a deck of French Tarot, dated approximately between the 14th and 15th centuries. However, the thing that amazed me as soon as I saw the display was the card normally referred to as the Ace of Rods, Spears or Wands, because in this deck, it was called the Ace of Bushrods and there in the middle of the card, as plain as day, was a hand painted picture of a bushrod. It was marvellous. I can't tell you how excited I felt. Needless to say, the owner was not interested in selling them to me.

When the time of my daughter's rite approached, I decorated the wand of the bushrod with brightly coloured ribbon wool which contained different shades of purple. I criss-crossed the ribbon down the whole length of the rod and then added a plait of my daughter's hair. I made the plait from hair taken from a ponytail that I had kept from her first ever haircut.

I attached the plait at the top of the rod and in doing so chanted my spell of intent:

Blood of my blood may you never forget
Always find the time to remember that the child within is always with you,
That your hopes, dreams and aspirations are protected, as is your spirit,
These are essential parts of who you are and therefore never far away even if you think you have lost them.
The message of this plait is to never forget who you are.

Next I attached three hawk feathers. 'Hawke' is my grandfather's name and therefore my mother's name also. This represented another ancestral link reminding my daughter of who she is and where she comes from and showing her the strength of her ancestral tribe that spans out behind her, giving her deep and strong roots from which to grow. I attached the feathers to the bushrod to signify that second thread of my daughter's ancestry but also as a reminder that she may be breath of my breath, but in truth, her breath is absolutely her own. As I tied them on, letting them hang at the side of the rod, I chanted my spell of intent:

Breath of my breath, may you always find the answers to your questions,
The courage to ask that which needs to be asked and therefore seek the answers with openness and integrity,
May you always have clear thought and clarity of mind along with the creativity and inspiration of the Awen,
May your dreams be full of magic and the truth of who you are,
Know that the birds are the messengers of the Gods and signify that your spirit is free and can fly just as easily as they do.
The message of the feathers is that you can be who ever you want to be.

Finally I attached a piece of animal bone as the third thread, onto which I carved the following three symbols: the waxing moon (depicting the maiden aspect and the phase of my daughter's life that she was preparing to embrace); the rune *Sol* (the Great Mother, to encourage her to step into her power and embrace the female fire energy); the sigil for the three ravens (the Crone and the wisdom of the ancestors, to remind her that she has the strength within her of all who have been before and although she is bone of my bone her body is her own, she is her own person). As I carved I chanted my spell of intent:

Bone of my bone, may you always find your inner joy and never lose the freedom of youth that is the spark of inspiration.
Know that the fire within will only get stronger as you grow and may that enable you to not fear the power of the sacred feminine.
May the wisdom of the ancestors never leave you for they course through your veins and in truth are part of you.
May you find your own wisdom in life and embrace all that you are. The message of the bone is that you have worth and are valued for being you.

After the bushrod was complete I made a little draw string bag with suede and leather cord. Into the bag I place herbs of lavender, rosemary, moss, frankincense and broom flowers. This represented additional protection and good health and would be worn around her neck for her challenge during the rite. I chanted my spell of intent as I sewed the pouch and then placed the herbs within:

Herbs of health and protection too, circle of fire, let your power be true.

I only had two more things to make in preparation for my daughter's rite of passage. I should add at this point, that in part, what I was doing was as much for me as it was for her; I too was going through a moving on process. This was my way of opening the door and stepping through into a different phase of my relationship with my daughter.

I next made a corn dolly from hay that I had bought from a pet shop. I bound the hay with green string, criss-crossing it to make the shape of the body and then attached the head and arms in the same way. I ragged the doll with the same ribbon wool I had used on the bushrod and hung small sprigs of moss, lavender, rosemary and an acorn around its neck. I did not chant over the doll because there was a specific purpose that the doll had been made for and it needed to be clear of pre-set intent.

The last thing I did was to collect a small piece of slate from Swithland Woods. Onto this I painted the sigil of the Triple Goddess, indicating Maiden Mother and Crone, the three aspects of the sacred feminine. Under this, finally, I drew the sigil of the waxing moon with the three rays of Awen beneath it, indicating *'To know Truth, To Love Truth and To Maintain Truth'*. This I would give to my daughter to add to the power pouch that she would take with her on her challenge.

So all my preparations were complete, but here is where we leave my daughter's rite of passage for I feel that it is a personal journey and not one that should necessarily be shared outside those who were present. Suffice to say the maiden is led ceremonially to face her challenge, knowing that when she returns and on completion of her set task, she will be welcomed into the House of the Mothers. As my own daughter was led away, as a priestess and just as importantly, as a mother I called out:

I call to you great Goddess, you of fire and water,
Great Mother of expectation, hopes and dreams,
Know this young warrioress
Fearless in her pursuit of life
Accept her personal sacrifice
Of moon-blood, full and red,
Let her feel the ebb and flow
Let her know the ebb and flow
Of creativity, fertility and of inspiration
The first steps of Awen swelling within
To know yourself
To love yourself
To maintain yourself
Young maiden feed your sprit and let it go
Know that you are truly free.

It's not always possible, however, for us to be able to be part of a big rite and we may not want to celebrate publicly or communally, but there are still things that can be done. There are rituals that have passed down through the ages and are now part of mainstream society, particularly if we think about the time of Imbolc, the festival of lactating ewes and the awakening of the Serpent Mother, which traditionally marks the birth of the Maiden and the spring time within the sacred Wheel of the Year, and Beltane, when it arrives, signifying the maiden's full transition into the Mother and summer.

As Imbolc is celebrated in the first few days of February, the winter is beginning to recede and we have a little more daylight. Traditionally, this was the time of the first spring clean, the sweeping out of winter after being closed up through the dark months. Our ancestors would have let the animals out, all old straw flooring cleared and burned and in later times all windows and doors opened to let in the fresh air.

The fireplaces were cleared and cleaned and then re-lit from the ritual fires. We have to be realistic that weather permitting, there might have been several major spring cleans between Imbolc and the Spring Equinox, but nonetheless, the idea of letting the light in was a ritual of importance after the harshness of the winter. I still make sure that I open all doors and windows, sweep all floors and clean out all of the fire places. This is also the time when I burn the evergreens that have decorated my hearth and home during the Yule festivities. I place a lit candle within all the fireplaces for the eve of Imbolc and then I relight my main hearth fire on Imbolc itself, but I always keep the candles burning in the fireplaces that I am not using in the house for three days following.

Other traditional celebrations that have continued uncloaked can be seen in the celebrations of Beltane now more commonly known as the May Day festivities: the phallic symbol of the sacred male stands large and erect in all its glory as the brightly coloured maypole, with the ribbons hanging down from it onto which young maidens and women hold on, dancing their weave of promised fertility. Interestingly my grandpy told me that they did not use ribbon, apart from the fact ribbon was far too expensive, instead it was ivy and evergreens which he said symbolised the continued fertility of the sacred male and that it was also a coming of age rite for young men who were now fertile and their seed plentiful.

Another rite celebrated at Beltane is the jumping of the fire. I personally find it bizarre that nowadays everybody, regardless of age and sex, jumps the fire if they want to. It is my understanding that this ritual was originally for the young women who wished for the fertility of the sacred male, represented by the heat of the fire, to be successful in impregnating them. I view the energy and the heat of the fire as representing the male passion rising and hardening in the throws of copulating with the women, thus confirming the intent of the young woman participating.

Maybe the young men held the circle, dancing and singing to the young women as they jumped, and maybe they also jumped. Perhaps it was a form of seduction, an open courtship whereby the young people had the opportunity to attract a mate, the young women demonstrating their courage as well as stating before the world that they were healthy, fertile and blessed by the Gods themselves, whilst the young men were shouting and dancing, showing off their prowess, their manhood, boasting of their abilities as warriors, hunters and providers as well as lovers.

However, just because we may have passed our maiden years and are now immersed in other phases of our life that doesn't mean that we cannot still honour this aspect of the Goddess and it does not mean that she becomes any less important to us and the cycle to which we are still part of as we struggle to find our place in the world and make sense of the life we lead and find the time to recognise the potential of what is and what might be waiting for us. Rituals and rites of passage, at designated and poignant times in our lives, enable us to come to terms, to make necessary changes, to honour our own accomplishments as well as those of others and therefore support us and enable us to find our own connection within and without. They give us the strength and courage to do what has to be done, to truly sing the song of self or the song of the tribe and of course the song of all things, thus enabling us, most importantly, to move forward.

As children we are so full of wonderment and expectation, we have no limitations and dreams are a reality. Because of that, and for an all too brief a time, perhaps we see the world as it truly is, full of magic and inspiration.

Babies and children are so aware of their senses with their survival mechanisms totally switched on and raring to go. Everything is about what they see, hear, smell, touch and taste, and they do not question why or deny what they see, hear, smell touch and taste, it just is. I think that for the most part we have lost touch with this more basic and essential core of ourselves. Perhaps we have been conditioned into ignoring that part of ourselves because it no longer conforms, is not considered acceptable and more worrying, is perceived as no longer needed as an essential component of us as individuals and humans within our modern world.

That, for me is one of the main gifts of the Maiden, the expectation of the new, the eternal wonderment I felt as a child, the never ending inspiration that fills us when we look forward to what is to come next. Life is an adventure and never boring. Perhaps life is also about accepting the need to reconnect with that basic and essential core of ourselves and recognise and acknowledge that some things just are, and not being conditioned into feeling that we always need to question or worse still, explain away.

JOURNEYING INTO THE CAVE OF THE MAIDEN

Part 1: The Journey
(Play back Part 1 taken from Chapter 1, or read out the transcript to assist you as you journey.)

To explore the internal Cave of the Dancing Maiden, to re-awaken the hope, inspiration and new beginnings that she can represent, we need not look too far, because it remains within us at all times as does the Maiden herself. Remember, the cave will be specific to you, it will show you what needs to be seen, it will represent whatever you need it to represents because it is and always will be part of you. Know that it represent the playfulness of youth, hope and inspiration, new beginnings and feeling invincible. It is the time of spring and all that might mean to you. It will hold your memories, dreams and aspirations that perhaps have lain forgotten until now or have yet to be born. So have no fear when you enter the cave because nothing can harm you there: instead it will be a place of laughter and lightness, a place to tap into the energy of youth, a place of freedom to boost yourself, and perhaps a special place to create and plan new and exciting projects yet to manifest in your life.

Part 2: Into the Cave
You are now stepping into your cave, the Cave of the Dancing Maiden. What wondrous things are kept within the cave of youth, dreams and inspirations? Remember the Maiden is an important part of you, she holds your innermost desires and the freedom to explore and grow. This is the place to think and plan and gather inspiration, to plant the seed of the coming year, month, week or days. This is a place to play, relax and be yourself free from prying eyes and looks of disapproval. Here you can be assured the freedom to dance and explore new concepts and forgotten dreams. So what do you see? How do you feel? Is there anyone else there? Spend as much time as you feel you need exploring and familiarizing yourself with the cave. Perhaps sit down awhile and meditate within the cave itself.

Part 3: The Return and Awakening
Use the transcript provided in Chapter 1. Return and awaken from your journey, happy and refreshed.

IMBOLC RITUAL

Part 1

For the ritual area we created three circles within each other, all lit with tea-light candles within brown bags half full of sand. These circles are the Circles of Gogyrwen the Primal Serpent Mother. The fire is set in the middle of the inner circle. This is an all night vigil and celebration. It is a time of women, by women, for women. This ritual can be adapted and made to fit your own requirements.

- Wait until dark with only the Gogyrwen circles lit along with the quarter torches. The main fire must still be unlit at this point.
- All women are masked.
- Process to the temple area, banging drums, singing, calling and chanting to the Mother Serpent/ Urdegan.
- The first call to the Goddess is made three times: *Yr Awen a ganaf, o dwfyn y dygaf. Seith ugein Ogyrwen, yssyd yn yr Awen* (from the Hostile Confederacy: Book of Taliesin) Translation: The Awen we sing, from the deep we bring it, seven score Gogyrwen are in the Awen.
- Welcome and call to the spirits of the land, to the serpents and the ancestors. (This will be the first explanation of the midwifing of the spring etc.).
- The calling of the quarters of earth, air, fire and water.
- The Priestess/ woman blesses the fire as she takes a flame and places it into the Imbolc pyre.
- Each person who called a quarter will take a light from their direction torch and give the blessings of the element to the Imbolc fire as they light it.
- The rest of the circle, one by one, will then take a light from the nearest flame and give their blessing to the Imbolc fire.

- Personal sacrifice of blood or wine (everyone has the opportunity to step forward).
- The blessing and sacrifice of Gogyrwen's three circles: the Circle of Acorns (the seed, the egg, the embryo, the potential of life); the Circle of Dew (the sacred sac, the nurturing waters of the mother, the protection and environment that enables life to grow); the Circle of Ewe's Milk (the nourishment to sustain life, the nurturing mother). In the centre of all is the sacred fire, the spirit, the spark of life that impregnates and engenders the beginning of all that we know as life.
- All the women now process around the three circles chanting and drumming. The chant is as follows: '*I am not afraid of the serpent, and the serpent is not afraid of me*'
- Once all have reach the Circle of the Acorn, the chanting becomes quiet as each will take an acorn as an offering to the fire and call out in return their wishes for the coming year.
- The chant is taken up again until the energy is raised and channelled into the fire.
- The Priestess will then open the circle without closing the ritual and so ends part one.

In-between Bit

- Feasting, dancing, singing, chanting, story telling and merriment now commences.
- The circle of women will write their own chant to birth the sun and thus the spring into being. This is the chant of the solar midwife.
- The fire must not be left unattended and must not be allowed to go out: feed it and honour it for the life force that it offers.

The Song of the Midwives: Part Two

- Places will be taken within the temple space and chanting will begin until the sun is re born.

- The spirits of place, the ancestors and Gogyrwen will be released but their gifts retained.

- The quarters will be closed

- The ritual ended.

Chapter 3
THE CAVE OF ILLUSION

Illusion
Falls the fool whose mind is closed
And emptiness fills the expanse called soul
Teetering on the edge of total destruction
Unaware of isolations, feelings of despair

Voices fall on deafened ears
And surround the world in painful silence
Ignorance pounds on skin-tight drums
As arrogance steals life's melodies

But when the storm breaks to reveal the view
The silence crashes, making way for the new
Then with an intake of breath I turn and I scream
For seldom is anything just what it seems.

The Gift of Life
I am in the mountains with snow covering everything around me except
for the rock faces that I can see in the distant. It is so cold, I am so cold,
there is a bitterly biting breeze cutting into my very being with every
icy breath it blows at me.

I begin to walk, unsure as to where I really am, what direction
I should take or even where I should be heading.

It is then that I see her as she slowly but deliberately walks toward me, an old lady with the most beautiful, wizened features, her slightly wavy silver-grey straw hair framing her face.

She is wearing skins and furs and a brightly coloured shawl wrapped tightly about her with her hood up and leather straps criss-crossing around the fur on her legs and a belt tied about her middle. She stops before me, with crystal clears eyes that penetrate deep inside me. I know and feel she is as old as the mountains and the land itself and yet as young as a bright green shoot pushing its way through the dirt to breathe in the air for the first time. I understand in that moment that she is all things and yet she is nothing.

From inside her shawl she retrieves a small package wrapped in many layers of white tissue paper.

"Take this gift from me…you are being given the gift of life". She says no more but continues to stand there with her hands outstretched with the gift sitting perfectly still in the palms of her hands.

Eventually I take the gift from her, thanking her as I do, still not really understanding what any of this means. I carefully unwrap the tissue from the gift that it hidden until I reach the final layer where, to my amazement, I find the most beautiful and delicate bird nest. Inside is a tiny little bird, lying on its side, very still and very dead.

"How awful" I cry, because in that moment such sadness has filled my heart. "Why would you give me a dead bird?" I cannot understand why such a thing could be called a gift.

"Not so" replies the old woman who has not once removed her eyes and focus from me. "She but sleeps. She has been dormant and hiding away. But now that you have pulled back the layers of tissue she will awaken to partake of life once more".

As the old woman speaks the little bird suddenly shakes itself onto its feet, ruffling and puffing out her feathers, singing her song out loud so that all will know she has returned.

"You see," says the woman, "you are like this bird, understand that she represents you. You also have been dormant, wrapped in tissue and hidden from the world. But now the tissue must be pulled away from you. It is time for you to wake up and take back your life. Hence this little bird represents the gift of life, and more importantly, your life".

With that the little bird flies up and out of the nest, she continues to sing to the world as she does so, up and away and eventually out of sight although I can still hear her song as though she were still within the nest.

I have no words for the old woman and I don't think any are expected for as quickly as she had arrived she is now gone and I stand once again alone but strangely warm and happy inside, I do not notice the cold biting wind this time as I sing to myself and the world around me.

I am a Druid Priestess, I am a witch, I am an Aquarian with Taurus Moon and Scorpio rising. I am a dreamer, a visionary, I am a shaman and I am a healer. I am all these things and so much more, I am a person, I am a woman and most importantly, I am an individual. The titles and gifts and abilities above are but aspects of me, natural and essential to my being. However, the names themselves are but shadows, names that are time specific, locality specific and conform to the acceptable face of society within accepted social norms. They are nothing but the smoke and mirrors, illusions and glamours by which I operate, function and survive, but they are still me.

Who you are and your personal preferences will determine what name you call me, but I will see no difference - they are all mirrors and I will always be who I am. A name is just that, a name, and you will give it as much or as little credibility as you wish. As we all know, from time to time, we can not help ourselves and we will judge others as we judge ourselves whether we realise it or not, thus acting as the self appointed mirror and that can be oh so very harsh.

Imagine, if you will, a circle within a circle within a circle, three rings of fire, hot, burning, pulsing and impenetrable, raging and spiralling and surrounding us. This represents the unmoveable force that governs our lives. These circles represent the necessities of our lives which will include our social interactions, families, friends, work, health issues and so on. They are the continuing circles of our lives and all connected within the eternal cycle of our personal lives' confines. The Cave of Illusion reflects our social and environmental conditioning, the boundaries and restrictions of our lives which are sometimes self-constructed and maintained. We provide the mirrors by which we identify ourselves, and our thoughts, actions and words are governed by that internal misrepresentation.

Within the cave we can gain clarity if we are prepared to smash away the illusions by challenging ourselves and learning to alter our perspectives from time to time. Rings of fire sound fierce and forbidding but perhaps that is part of the illusion, after all fire is strength and passion, belief and an energy that warms, it supports life and burns away the dead wood so that the new may grow.

Life Experience

How do we define ourselves? Over the years I have felt like I was everything other than Michelle, woman and individual. I am a mother, wife, lover, partner, daughter, sister, friend, priest, artist, counsellor - the list goes on and on. It took me a very long time to realise that the Michelle who had disappeared was there all the time and had never actually left me. I had redefined my boundaries so that I could fit in with all the roles that were important to me and made me feel needed. This identified who I was to others whilst providing me with a powerful shield to hide behind.

My world was definable, manageable (or so I thought); I had perfectly legitimate reasons why I couldn't do certain things that I wanted to, why I couldn't go to art college and study fashion design in London, why I couldn't travel, why I hadn't followed any of my personal dreams which I instead allowed to fester inside me. I am a mother I told myself, I'll have to wait until the children are at school or have grown to independence so that I can follow the dream career that I had always wanted. I'm the wife of a sick husband with a congenital and degenerative condition that has affected him all his life, which is why he drinks so much and treats me and his family so poorly, but I cant possible expect him to support my needs when his are so important and he needs me. Then I didn't go to university when I was younger, I got pregnant very young and lets be fair, I'm not really that academic so perhaps it was for the best, although I felt I let my parents down badly and that I had always been a big disappointment to them (this was not the reality, as I found many years later). And so it goes on and on, you get the picture. However, whilst there were many circumstances outside of my control the illusion that I was powerless to do other than what I was actually doing, that was still just an illusion, one due to conditioning, circumstance, defences, inappropriate coping strategies and more often than not, youth. Regardless, illusion it was and the boundaries I set reflected what others could see but I could not.

Head up Michelle, now walk tall and proud, shoulders back, send your energy out as you walk, let them see what you want them to see, and let them see what they expect to see. I can't remember how old I was when this 'game' began. Dressed up in fabulous velvets, make-up, feathers and beads, my grandma and I played the 'glamour' game. It is nobility that you must show, and if you are small let them see you as big, if you are short let them see you as tall and when the need arises pull your energy in, and don't let them see you at all (though I have always struggled with that last one). Walk with the gait of a priestess, a princess, a person of importance: it is illusion, smoke and mirrors. It is part of the magic of being whoever and whatever you want or need to be in this or any other world, regardless of what others might think is happening. I would practice for hours walking up and down the hall with grandma, and we would have afternoon tea and sandwiches or scones, jam and cream; it was a special time, magical with lessons that I have never forgotten even if I forget to use them from time to time.

The Three Circles of Fire

The three circles of fire can determine our actions and the practical application of those actions within the self-imposed boundaries that we have constructed affecting us on our life's journey. However, there is, I feel, another aspect of the three rings of existence that are just as important to our growth and it is the connecting of mind, body and spirit with the realms of land, sea and sky which can also be viewed as the three realms of being, both physically and spiritually.

Gogorwen (the serpent goddess I mentioned in the last chapter) also has three rings of power with ritual offerings at the time of re-birth at the fire festival of Imbolc. In the centre of the circles is the Imbolc fire, representing the eternal flame, the spark of life of the God that impregnates and fertilises the seed or egg of the Goddess.

The first circle of Gogorwen is the egg, the seed and the spirit. A circle of acorns surround the fire, the God spark in the centre. The acorns represent the inspiration, that which has yet to be born but is ready to be conceived, the potential that all things (ideas, dreams, ambitions) however small and undeveloped or remote they may seem, can be, given the right spark, ignited into being. So this gives you an opportunity to think about what you want to do next, what great adventure, dream or focus do you want in your life? Plant the seed and let it grow.

The second circle that encompasses the circle of acorns is the Ring of Dew. The dew is collected at dawn from grasses, flowers and leaves. These crystal gems of nature are sustenance, saving all who drink from thirst - the thirst of unfulfilled dreams and ambitions, a thirst which can lead to stunted growth and even death. The dew comes from the sacred womb of the Mother providing the waters of life that protect and enable safe growth, feeding all of our aspirations, enabling birth and life renewed. This circle reminds us of what is important in life - that we need to look after ourselves; that it is important to be held and even contained at times within boundaries. It shows us that, when appropriate, limitations can offer sustainability that can protect and defend, but at the same time are also flexible and enable movement, growth and development in a safe, relaxed and secure environment. We are made up of over two thirds water, it is sacred from the moment we are conceived and held within our mother's womb, right through to our deaths. It is our elixir and as essential as of all of the other elements to our continued existence, health and well being.

The third circle that surrounds the two other rings is a ring of ewe's or mother's milk. Once new life has breathed its first breath it must be feed and nurtured, nourished with the goodness of the mother's milk which will add its own ring of protection and, as with the ewe's milk, also introduces the new life to the practical skills and knowledge of personal need, care and understanding for growth and development and the independence of will to follow it through.

With the gift of bringing new life into the world and enabling the growth of firm roots to hold that life strong in whatever storms might befall it (as well as encouraging the strength and determination to succeed) it is important to recognise that this is as relevant to the life of a child as well as any projects, dreams and aspiration that you have identified within the other two circles. Be ready to allow one or two sparks from the flame of the sacred God fire to ignite, fertilise and give meaning and spirit to them.

It is always difficult to see the wood for the trees, so how do we identify ourselves? Why do we set ourselves limitation, labels and boundaries which can restrict and even hide who we really are? There are so many factors that contribute including upbringing, learned behaviour, social conditioning, economics and environment. However, sometimes it is good to challenge ourselves and the boundaries of how we identify and value ourselves. It can be an emotional journey and one that is difficult and painful but it can also be a magical awakening, a journey of personal empowerment, liberation and perhaps the *eureka* moment of the stark realization of an absolute truth.

Within this chapter I am sharing a ritual that I have used time and time again. You can adapt it if you prefer to experience this on your own, however, but it is an amazing one to share with others. You can make it as elaborate or as simple as you like to fit your needs at any given time.

THE RITUAL OF SELF TRUTH

In our ever busy lives it can become easy to lose ourselves in the mundane complexities of day to day living. We often identify ourselves by who we are within our families, friendships, work environments and communities and seldom do we identify with just being who we are. This exercise is to show you the truth, because at the end of the day that is all that we have left.

1. Write down on separate pieces of paper seven of the most important things which you believe define who you are and your accomplishments, this could be your partner, children or work etc.

2. Once you have written down your seven most important things, number them according to a sliding scale of importance with 1 being the most important.

3. Now light a small fire or a candle but ensure you have a place that is safe to work. Once this has been done take the piece of paper with the least important thing by which you identify yourself. It should be numbered 7, and then acknowledging that aspect of you place into the flame and burn it.

4. Continue to give to the flame your pieces of paper until you are left with the most important one to you, which should be numbered 1. Think about all that you have already put into the fire, think about what it means to put this last one into the fire, to discard that label and identity and think about what is

left. Then as with the others, give your last and most important identity to the fire and let it burn.

5. You have chosen to rid yourself of the labels and the identities that have shaped you, given your life meaning, limited you or helped you grow, and yet here you still are, the same person, no older, no younger, but what is the truth that you are left with?

6. Turn and face a mirror - for that in truth is what you are left with! That's right *you*. Even if those things no longer existed, the things that you burned, even if they are still as important to you as when you started this exercise, the point is at the end of the day they are *not* you. They are but aspects, they do not define you; *you* define you. You are the initiator and you are the creator, you have control of your life and what you do within that life. Ultimately you have ownership of you.

When I last carried out this exercise as part of a workshop, the women found it very difficult to burn the pieces of paper in my cauldron. As each woman carried out the ritual on their own the others were left wondering what was happening. After they had burned their bits of paper, they were blindfolded to face the truth. One by one they were led into a sacred area and placed on their hands and knees with their heads facing the ground. Then, and only then, were they allowed to see the truth that was all that was left to them. The blindfold removed, what they saw was their own reflection in the mirror beneath them, a very powerful experience for most of the women, acknowledging that they are the truth of who they truly are and not the other things that whilst all terribly important for whatever reason, still aren't who they are. That is a very valuable thing to remember.

JOURNEY INTO THE CAVE OF ILLUSION

Part 1: The Journey
(Play back Part 1 taken from Chapter 1, or read out the transcript to assist you as you journey).

As you explore the internal Cave of Illusion, think about the many boundaries and limitations that have affected you all of your life. This is the cave of mirrors, enabling you to see yourself as you truly are. This is the cave of the creator and the initiator and you are that person, the creator and initiator of your own life. Remember, the cave will be specific to you, it will show you what needs to be seen, it will represent whatever you need it to represent because it is and always will be, part of you. The Cave of Illusion represents the boundaries that we have placed upon ourselves. It is our social conditioning and the limitations by which we live our lives. Remember, a ring, within a ring, within a ring. But how does all of this manifest for you?

Part 2: Into the Cave
Once within your cave walk around, familiarize yourself with it and see what there is to see. Is everything as it should be? Are there any differences? Try to take note of as much as you can but don't allow it to become the focus for this journey.

What do you see? How do you feel? Is there anyone else there? Spend as much time as you feel you need. How does it make you feel and what insights do you think there are to be gained here? What if anything needs to be added, changed, and moved? Most importantly, how do you see yourself in this cave in relation to your everyday existence?

So when you are ready perhaps sit down awhile, meditate within the cave itself. Ask for help and guidance if that is what you feel you need. It is really up to you. There are no rules within your cave except the ones that you impose.

Part 3: The Return and Awakening

Use the transcript provided in Chapter 1. It is helpful to record it then play it back or have someone read it out to enable you to return and awaken from your journey, happy and refreshed.

Chapter 4
THE CAVE OF VEILS

I am the water carrier
Eccentric in the sun
For I am of air, vapours in the sky,
Mystic of the zodiac
Of forward sight and inner vision
I see myself in rainbow colours
In shades of blues, purples, reds and greens
That merge together for all to see.

With the moon,
She grounds my fears
And brings out my bullish horns of earth and greens
She gives me my freedom and keeps me safe
And locks away my hidden self,
From all who want to see.

The sting of the scorpion's tail
Lashes out whenever I least expect
Bringing out all of my strength and passion
My desperation and pain in all its rage
In the waning of the moon.

For I am the water carrier
Unpredictable to all I know

I never do what I am supposed to
I never allow anyone too near
For I am of air, vapours in the sky,
Of greenest earth and waterfalls
In shades of blues, purples, reds and greens
That merge together for all to see.

Look out of your personal turret windows dear ones, from way up high and take in the view as you do. Look out across the clouds and the mountains and the sacred lands of the Gods of yesteryear and know they still draw near. Magic, shadows and illumination will guide your vision and show you all that there is to see…all that you can see…all that you want to see.

Lift the mists of your mind and see the world, your world through the awed eyes of a prism lens, splintered images, the possibilities of different realities and truths all dancing and hanging in the air just like the crescent moon.

How do you see me in all my truth and glory? How do you see yourself whilst enabling others to see you in their turn? Into the Cave of Veils I bid you go, because I am here, there and everywhere; I am the insight, the depth, the inspiration and the intellect; I am the perspective cradled and held within crystal sights and perspective that can be shrouded and altered by veils, masks and obstacles of chance and design.

I am the internal voice of understanding, reason and knowledge; I am the internal voice of deception, ignorance and intolerance which you can hide behind, self-empowering or self-destructive.

How many shades tint your view? Oh come on dear ones, how do, or should you, see the view, the very images before your eyes?

Intuition, visions and divination are natural tools for natural needs and are all natural abilities. Your truth, your sight, your understanding may differ from mine; your truth won't always be my truth but look where we stand; you seen and me unseen, you on one side of a fence whilst others remain on theirs.

So shape-shifter and walker between worlds, natural chameleon, diplomat, protagonist, or wager of war, which mask do you wear today and who do you wear it for?

It is good to remember that all things shift and change, because that is the natural order of things. So what will you see tomorrow regardless of whether your eyes are open or closed? And while you contemplate this, think upon whose door it will lead you to.

Oh, distorted world through prism specs, of veiled vision on a never-ending wave of changing tides. Who are you? How do you see your world and how does the world see you in return?

Lifting the Veil

There is no point in crying over dreams that can never be and yet the craft enables focus on such things, showing us that with careful thought and total belief, anything is possible.

So here I am weaving my web of words and images, carefully placing the fractured elements of my visions together, piece by piece, and as the picture becomes clearer so does the intent, the need and the desire. So be careful what you wish for, it just might come true, but then that's the point... isn't it?

We are fragile in our understanding and perceptions, forever shaped by an ever-changing world, victims, perhaps, of circumstance and yet viewed as willing participants to others who look on.

We are the result of our upbringing, environment, the wider social norms, peer groups, communities and our personal experience, and so much more. How do we manage so many diverse and multi-faceted aspects? How do we allow ourselves to look beyond the veil, to challenge, to be pro-active enabling positive change and movement? It is necessary for us to wear many 'hats' during our day to day life. Who we are, how we interact and how we are perceived will differ and will be dependant upon which hat we are wearing at any given time.

The Cave of Veils holds all of our diverse and changing hats. It sometimes reminds me of *Mr Ben's* magic changing room. I always got excited as a child wondering who he would become after entering the magic shop and its changing room but the truth is, the veils of our lives, the hats that we wear and the masks that we create are important to us. They protect us and enable us to step outside our comfort zones, they provide an opportunity to leave the mundane behind and step into a different reality and are a natural part of our existence.

Who is truly behind the layers of veils, hats and multi-faceted masks? The veils can hide the reality of things or act as a means of delineating the boundaries between what can be seen and what is unseen. The veils between the worlds can lift and be parted into that place of mystery, inspiration and dreams, providing us with understanding, vision, knowledge and empowerment.

Seers, both ancient and modern, understand the concept of the veils, the shades and tints they cast in their shadow and this is part of the study and practice of navigating these often hidden ways. Divination, intuition, prophecy and ritual are all held within, behind and under the veils. As well as hats and masks, the treasures of self can be accessed and utilised with perception and perspective. All of us use these skills without even realizing we do so in our daily lives, in all of our decision making processes, in our concepts, plans and their implementation. All of this is natural magic and a manifestation of what is essential and natural to us.

Magic

I have been told on many an occasion that magic doesn't really exist and is therefore just an ego trip by those of us who say it does. I can't understand this argument at all. My understanding is that magic is knowledge. There is no mystery other than what that knowledge contains how it is understood and used.

I was challenged on this very issue not so very long ago when I was told, during a very heated debate, emphatically, that magic could not and does not exist. The evidence to support this statement was asserted as fact because I, it had been noted, have no personal power over the sun staying up in the sky or on its daily rising and setting. I therefore have no magical impact on anything at all. Ho, hum I say to myself, they are missing the big point! It is not about claiming or actually being able to keep the sun up in the sky or getting it to rise or set at my bidding, this is a ridiculous thing to say. Instead it is, as far as I am concerned, about recognising, seeing and connecting to the universal energy that does.

We all have energy and generate energy. The magic is in how we use, focus and manipulate that energy. The magic is in understanding that we are part of it and it is part of us, and it is through our intent that we are able to direct ourselves both physically and energetically, manifesting that which is required in order for us to thrive and develop. Let's be clear here, I do not and cannot and never have had control over the sun. This is because the sun sings its own song and moves to its own music. However, I can respond, I can connect and I can utilize that energy, even if it is only on the level of getting my daily dose of vitamin D.

I do not understand why the concept of magic is feared and so controversial. Magic is my personality, it's my energy, it's what makes me and highlights my individuality. It is not abstract, it is tangible and a measurable commodity by the very fact that I am alive, it is as natural as anything else on this or any other world. So why, I ask again, deny it? To do so is, in my mind, just denying an essential and natural part of yourself and the world you live in. In a world governed by science and logical explanation, it would seem that our need is still governed by the motivation of necessity, in what ever form that might take and is, for the most part, never far away.

Ritual
The need for ritual and ritualisation is perhaps one of the most basic human instincts. Ancestors from all over the globe have ritualised

their way of life and the beauty or horrors that it held with ceremonies honouring of the tribe, the community, the dead and the land, creating places of remembrance, celebration and learning, opening doorways and building bridges between the living and the dead, the seen and the unseen.

It can be argued then that ritual and ritualisation was (and still is) about self preservation, personal and communal development through focused intent and manifestation.

Ritual is a tool. It lets people know who they are, who we are, what our understanding is and what our needs are. Our customs and rituals can be thought of as an essential part of our identity, culturally and personally, highlighting all of our similarities and all of our differences.

Magically, ritual provides the focus and the structure. It is the key that can unlock the door into other worlds of reality, as well as providing insight, perspective and growth in this reality. Ritual, by definition, cannot be static in its form. It is not uniform in its appearance. It is diverse, organic, creative, inspirational and insightful. In short, it mirrors who we are, our needs at any given time be it in service to others or in pursuit of personal survival, development and clarity.

The language of ritual is about identifying and belonging, feeling comfortable and safe, albeit challenging and stimulating. It is about clarity of thought and deed, intent and focus and it most definitely is, in my opinion, a statement of self and service.

If we look at ritual and celebration, they are not necessarily mutually exclusive, although they are often thought of as being one and the same. We have our normal daily rituals, for example the business of going to work. Even on the day of the office party all of the official business of the day is concluded before the party begins. Ritual is the business, the time to do what needs to be done, regardless of the circumstances, be it joyful or sorrowful. The celebration and *Gorsedd* is the coming together afterwards with socialising and rejoicing.

A misconception is in the nature of 'performing' ritual. There are elaborate and even 'officially' recognised models of practice, in terms of where, when and how. But is all of this necessary? Well yes and no, depending on what you are doing and why you are doing it (and of course personal safety). However, ritual is about adaptability and therefore the whole world is your altar and the key is to recognise and identify where, when and how. Ritual is diverse, varied in conception and subjective in perception and meaning. Each of us will have our own understanding and preferred method of construction and participating in ritual.

Over the years I have been part of small gatherings as well as huge extravaganzas. Personally I love big rituals that are full of pageantry with all the colour and spectacle that they can offer - if the content and intent is clear and has appropriate focus I don't see the problem. I see major value within these types of rituals just as much as the smaller, more intimate and closed rites. I view the pageantry of open ritual as an opportunity to bring community together in a symbolic and ritualistic way. It offers us, as priests, the means to create and hold a sacred space that opens doorways that can affect all of us with ritual spectacle that stimulates and challenges mind, body and spirit. We are working together to create a safe arena for those who are, perhaps, new to craft and ritual or who are more used to solitary practice, as well as those of us for those more used to this form of practice. As priests we may act as conduits holding the space but most importantly we facilitate and open an accessible porthole that enables all who want to to walk between the worlds. Ritual helps us to create an alternative reality and a place of liminality via a metaphoric bridge that all can cross. This is a place to step outside the mundane, and have a truly personal and communal experience.

Having said all of the above, I am just as happy working within a small, closed group where ritual has the opportunity to be less generalized and perhaps more intense in its focus and intent. I could also apply those thoughts to my solitary practice, because always it is all about what is appropriate and needed at any given time.

Ritual is so personal an area within our spiritual practice that it truly is 'each to their own' but perhaps reading this will open a debate that explores the idea that just as our life experiences are different our needs often differ, and this will manifest and be reflected in what rituals we choose to do and when and how we choose to do them.

I have journeyed a lot recently to inspire me in my writing and enable me to express myself and share my craft and Druidry as I understand it. Interestingly the thing that repeated itself to me was the need to follow the path signposted with *Truth*, acknowledging that it does not necessarily follow that your truth will match that of others or indeed will be accepted and understood. Truth is always about perspective and, it could be argued, subjective.

This was certainly apparent in the mythical aura of 'truth' that I always saw wrapped tightly around my grandmother. She was, in every sense of the word, a living, walking dichotomy. To many my grandma was a hateful, spiteful and nasty woman who was a troublemaker, impossible to work with or live next door to, let alone be related to. She was considered unpredictable and contrary with what might now be considered a well developed personality disorder. Sadly she was, to many, all of these things and more. However behind this veil and well crafted mask I saw and knew a different woman.

She was amazingly intelligent, gifted, creative, magical and inspirational, a weaver of tales and fascinating stories, an artist of wonderful abilities and hidden depths, a generous woman, eccentric and as mad as a box of frogs. She had a tremendous sense of humour and absolutely no tolerance for those she considered idiots. Grandma was thoughtful insomuch as she understood what made each of us tick and what was important to us. That didn't mean that she acted on that insight with everyone, but for those of us that she did, she supported, nurtured and fed those aspects.

Everything was magical and exciting. She believed in the seen and unseen and she didn't care. Having said all of that, she was very lonely a lot of her life, never seeming to make friends easily and, from what I can gather, this was true for her even as a child. Thus her world became a magical one, a world where her dolls existed as living entities, where her stories were full of adventure, and the Fair Folk played with her and told her their secrets. All of these things were as real to her as anything else in her life. There always remained a childlike quality to her. Many who knew her will most likely disagree with me, but I don't care, because this is my grandma, and this is who she was to me. I am not them and therefore will never see grandma through their eyes and they, well they are most assuredly are not me and will never see her through my eyes either.

In following our truth we admit our aspirations and maybe recognise for the first time that they exist at all. I believe that in some way our aspirations can be interpreted as reflections of our higher self and can be achievable and realistic goals to set ourselves.

Ultimately we are seeking enlightenment. By starting with ourselves we naturally become more aware of who and what we are. This results in an increased awareness of all around us and our organic interaction and our intertwined existences but it has been my experience that one of the hardest lessons to learn is that of acceptance and I have found that the Craft/Druidry can be used as a tool in this endeavour. By the very nature of acceptance, we should recognise and consider it as an ongoing process which should not be constricted by boundaries and one that will ultimately mean different things at different times and therefore cannot be and indeed is not, a static force.

Visualization Exercise

In the sacred space that you have created for yourself, light a candle. Relax and sit staring deep into the flame in front of you. As you do become aware of your breathing; allow it to become slow and rhythmic, in and out, deep and gentle, never taking your eyes from the flame. Relax your body as you continue to meditate on the candle and on the flame, allowing your mind to clear of all your day to day concerns, worries and activities. Once you have done this just allow yourself to gently form the image of the candle that you know is in front of you, in your mind's eye.

Take your time, there is no rush, but when you feel ready close your eyes but keep the image of the flame in front of you in your mind's eye. Don't worry if the image fades away quickly at first, just open your eyes and begin the process again. The more you practice the easier it will become. Try for 10 -15 minutes a day.

As you become more confident with this exercise, try other objects and in time move to a complete scene, for example, your garden or a room. See the detail, walk around it in your mind's eye. Note down what stands out, what you missed, what was added or left out and even what it felt like. Try to use all of your senses and see what you discover. Remember this exercise is a gateway to journeying and will enhance your perceptive abilities.

JOURNEYING INTO THE CAVE OF VEILS

Part 1: The Journey
(Play back Part 1 taken from Chapter 1, or read out the transcript to assist you as you journey).

Think about your dreams and aspirations, what has helped or hindered you. The Cave of Veils is a place of intellect and thought. It is liminal and expansive; by definition there can be no limits other that those we place upon ourselves.

What are your perspectives, your personal agendas? How do you see yourself and others in their turn? Are you afraid to lift the proverbial lid to see what is inside? And perhaps ask yourself 'is it time to put on those cosmic specs so that your world, the universe and all things can take on a new existence and meaning.

Perhaps it will become a place of contemplation, of respite or of gathering hidden knowledge for you, a library of infinite possibilities and resources. Ultimately it will be what you need it to be, it will become a place of relevance to you at any given point in time, never static, always organic and open to all possibilities.

Part 2: Into the Caves

I cannot describe what you will find and what you will see when you enter the Cave of Veils because that is your world but know it as a place of thought and reason, of ideas, intellect, insight and knowledge. How that chooses to manifest for you will depend upon you and your experiences, perspectives and your needs. What masks and veils will you find and have you hidden there?

Recognise the cave as being yours in all aspects, as are all the caves, and utilise its gifts in the way that suits you best. This is the place where you can gather and store knowledge, retrieving it as and when it is required. Ask for guidance, divine and seek that which might be thought lost, is needed or needs to be understood. Immerse yourself in all that it has to offer and embrace all that it has to give, acknowledging the wisdom that is the Cave of Veils.

Part 3: The Return and Awakening

Use the transcript provided in Chapter 1. Awaken from your journey happy and refreshed.

CREATING YOUR OWN SYSTEM OF DIVINATION

I find divination to be personally specific. Each of us has our own internal language and interpretation of images, situations and ideology, all of which make up some of the tools necessary when devising our own method of divination.

This exercise will very much be about you and what you identify with. There is no right or wrong way of creating your own method and tools of practice and it does not need to make sense to anybody apart from you. What you are creating is your own personal window into what needs to be seen in a personal language of interpretation that is all your own.

I am a great believer that anything can be used as a tool of divination, be it beer mats (yes I have given readings using beer mats!), tarot, runes, shells, etc. They are providing focus, a window of intent and vision into an altered sense of reality. It is from here that you can then gain the required insight.

Here is an example of one of my own divinatory sets. All of the items that make up this particular set have been gathered over many years or were given to me as gifts and all have meaning to me. They are an eclectic collection with no significance or value except to me, and yet each one provides an invaluable addition to my divinatory practice and my insight. I have provided my personal interpretations for the items I've used. Some of them you might agree and some of them you might feel something different about it and that's okay. Regardless of what manner of divinatory tools you are using, the interpretations that are provided should *only* be viewed as a guideline and are therefore not absolute.

My eclectic little bag of tricks can be used in a variety of ways: people can pull an item from the bag which can be used as a form of oracle, or they can pull several which can then be placed upon a prepared layout. Then the intuitive nature of divination needs to come into play. See beyond the objects themselves, take notice of images, feelings and even sounds that come into your mind's eye and always remain focused on the context of the reading and interpret what you see accordingly. Have fun, experiment, be considerate and be responsible in how you use them and who you use them for.

A Large Natural Ring of Shell: It is not even, nor is it a perfect circle of shell, but then nether are the boundaries and limitations that we place upon ourselves in life. Look at the boundaries surrounding you. Are there to few or are there to many? Perhaps security with flexibility is needed or perhaps a sanctuary or place of personal safety is required. The key is to understand that for the most part we are responsible for our own limitation and our own state of being.

Old, Large Mother of Pearl Button (This button is at least 100 years old and it is hand made): Just because we have to deal with the practicalities and complexities we face in life, this doesn't mean that we should be blind to the beauty of everyday things, individuals and situations. Perhaps we need to be more practical in our approach to specific issues or individuals, or perhaps we need to stop making life so difficult for ourselves because simplicity that is tried and tested is more often than not the way to go.

Owl Claw: The claws of any bird of prey are designing to hold on and not let go. There are times in our lives when we need to do likewise. Maybe there is a need to hunt for what is needed to sustain you in your life and in doing so utilise the knowledge and skills that already exist within. There is wisdom in being true to yourself and not trying to be anything other than who you are; personal development will always follow you in your flight of life. Don't be afraid of the dark, embrace it for there is much nourishment, wonder and wisdom to be gained.

Fox Bone: Foxes have a reputation for being shy and crafty and yet they are so resourceful. Maybe that slyness is thoughtfulness and there is a master strategist at work and perhaps that craftiness denotes a creature that understands its environment, the nature of other living things and therefore knows what needs to be done and when it needs to be done. Just maybe all of these things need to be considered in our own lives - a little more awareness, fewer hasty and rash decisions and caution until all facts can be assessed. Be clever, don't be naïve, be resourceful and act when you know it is right to do so and retreat when you know it is right to do so.

Tiger's Eye Crystal: Camouflage and blending in with those about you are marvellous abilities but not if you are suppressing your own needs and desires. This might be the point you have reached and now you need to stand on your own two feet. Have strength and conviction in your own knowledge and abilities, stand and fight for what is right and have the courage to move forward, making any necessary changes that might be required. Of course life is always about balance, so camouflage and blending in might be the courageous thing to do.

Limpet Shell: Sometimes we need to be unmoveable in our position regardless of what life throws at us. The limpet withstands the storms of the sea without flinching as it remains firm in its place upon the rock. However, sometimes we may need to consider that we are being stubborn and stuck in our ways, and understand that we need to compromise or move. Being firm and uncompromising has its place but we need to be aware that there is always the law of cause and effect and such behaviour can become detrimental to us and those around us.

Mermaid's Purse: From the mermaid's purse comes new life and transformation. It is a place of new beginnings, the spark of life. Now may be the time to follow your dreams to renew any aspirations and ambitions you may have harboured but have yet to act upon. Transformation can be for good or bad - which way is it taking you? Enjoy the gift of life and perhaps focus on what inspires you to realise your full potential.

Clear Quartz Crystal: We all need clear vision and to see things for what they are. Crystal can sometimes give us a distorted view, a rainbow view, but mostly it provides a pure channel through which we can see. This can be cathartic, this can be distressing, but it is a time of truths not illusions and this can be perhaps the start of a healing energy needed to put things into perspective.

Small Bottle of Sacred Earth (made up of earth from all the places I have lived and the sacred sites of Britain special to me): All of us need roots to hold us, feed us, nurture us and protect us and these can be found in the earth beneath our feet, the paths walked by our ancestors and within the very place we call home. This little bottle of earth represents the need for security, for hearth, home and family to be considered. Maybe there is need for a sense of belonging, to settle down and feel connected to those about you. Mind, body and spirit are the important factors that need nurturing and feeding by creating a place of peace and wellbeing.

Shark Tooth: Sometimes we need to be direct and not indecisive. However, we also need to know when enough is enough. Sharks can be intimidating even when they don't mean to be. Sharks can have a feeding frenzy and will carry on until there is nothing left. Sharks do not think about the consequences outside of their own needs. There is a time to act ruthlessly and a time to stop and show compassion. There is a need to remember that with great success can come great pain, be it directly to you or the fallout to others about you.

Driftwood: Are you drifting through life riding the crest of the wave? Is there need for direction and focus? Have you been washed upon the shore, worn, abandoned and feeling unloved? Or do you view yourself as seasoned wood, enjoying time out, allowing the waves of life to take you on the next big adventure? Maybe now is the time to have purpose in your life even if that means being freer from the normal constraints of your day to day life.

Dice: Life can be unpredictable; sometimes our path can appear hidden and life can feel like a throw of the dice, all in the hands of the fates. Sometimes we are just not meant to know, and sometime the unexpected happens to turn our world around. Maybe you are trying too hard to control everything, covering all the bases, trying to eliminate the element of surprise and chance, although maybe, just maybe, you have been gambling too much and have lost control. From time to time we need that surprise, we need the fates to take control and show us the way. Perhaps every now and then throwing the dice and seeing where it lands is a good thing.

Blue John Stone: Nothing is gained without sacrifice. We can reap the rewards for hard work done but we must not procrastinate or expect others to always carry the load for us. Just as the miners crawled under the ground with their picks and shovels, grafting for hours and hours to find the beautiful and valuable Blue John stone, so must we in our lives so that we to can reap the harvest of our endeavours. All is achievable and within your reach if you are prepared to put in the effort, time and energy.

Small Amethyst Wand: Directing a wand enables the user to focus their energy in whatever is required at that moment of time in a safe and protected way. Amethyst provides protection and encourages personal development. So have confidence in yourself and what you do, in what you want to do and in what you might have already achieved. Focus and direct you attentions in the right areas and don't be concerned with others' opinions. You can manifest your own reality: see it, be it and do it.

Hazel Nut: All things start from seed-like states, but within that seed lies a wealth of knowledge, wisdom and potential. Don't try to run before you can walk. All good things come to he who waits and if is worth doing, it is always worth doing well. So if we water, feed and nurture our seed it will grow strong and healthy, striving to become the best that it can be. We don't always need to rush and perhaps taking our time will be more productive for us.

Very, Very Old Key (This key belonged to my great grandma and it was an old key then. It was handed down and was eventually given to me by my grandma): A key can unlock many things, be it doors, problems or physical and physiological issues, but in return it can also lock things away, hiding them from sight, allowing things to be lost and forgotten. So do you need to remember that there is nothing so terrible that will not pass, cannot be opened and cannot be solved?

That for things to remain hidden, lost or even forgotten may mean more harm than good? Or is it that there is a time and a place for things to be put away, remembered perhaps but not so influential as to hold you back? We are never as trapped as we may first imagine because we have the key required or we *are* the key that is required - either way the key is always the answer.

Chapter 5
THE CAVE OF DUELLING SERPENTS

I am nourishment
I am poison
I am.
(M. Axe 07)

.

The food you eat can either be the safest and most powerful or the
slowest form of poison. (Ann Wigmore)

Tightly coil the serpents about my person, squeezing and pulling me
this way and that. Flicking their tongues, caressing my face, penetrating
their venom in to the dark recesses of my mind, never leaving me,
never letting go and always trying to ensure that their embrace
continues its hold, continues is control and continues to drain me in
ways that can not be imagined. An eternal conflict with one another
for the dominance of me, my life and my choices because that which
nourishes also poisons.

My throat is dry, the words fail to fall from my lips, my
frustration in not being heard or understood. I lack the confidence to
act and I shy away from that which must be or needs to be done. Oh,
I have excuses aplenty to fill the void, I have more reason than most,
I tell myself, and so the inappropriate coping strategies replace the
chasm that has opened up within.

But then my thoughts and words take form, spewing forth in
a torrent, lashing those about me, enforcing their meaning, perhaps in

anger, frustration, excitement or with authority. An avalanche upon those who see me, hear me and watch me. I have overwhelmed them, maybe even offended them, my meaning, my intent is lost. I've gone too far; there was no measure in my actions, thoughts and deeds and I have perhaps set myself, my cause and my life back by the excesses and extremes I had no understanding of and no control over.

The serpents of pleasure and pain, of communication, expansion of energy and transformation continue their endless work. For them there is no right and wrong, there are no limits, no boundaries and no excuses. They represent all that is good for us and all that is bad, the light and the dark, and there cannot be one without the other. Instead they promote personal development, personal responsibility and personal growth. The magic of the serpents, their secret message and the key, can be known as 'balance in all things'.

Too much of a good thing is bad, just as not enough is bad, but we live in a world of excesses; we perhaps have lost our self discipline, and often we are all too quick to refuse to take responsibility for the choices we make.

The Duelling Serpents

So into the cave of the duelling serpents, a cave of wonders and colour, filled to the top with all of the treasures that we love, need, want, hate and fear: A cave of delights, of chocolate, cakes and other fabulous rich foods. A feasting table of unbelievable delights and unlimited resources, never empty no matter how much we fill our plates and eat, and lets be fair here, how could one leave such delights without sampling them all, stuffing our faces until we are unable to move? Oh yes, how many times can we go back to the table and fill our plates ensuring in our heads that we are always getting our money's worth, regardless of whether or not we have paid or not. If we are honest, we all know that nothing is free in this world and pay we always do, because all of us know deep down that the law of cause and effect always comes into play and more often than not money will have nothing to do with it.

The duelling serpents of our existence can be felt in every essence of our being. The duality that is present within all aspects of life, whether it is manifest in night and day, man and woman or summer and winter, can be seen, felt, touched and tasted, in all aspects of our day to day lives whether we realise it or not.

The internal serpents of pain and pleasure, need and greed, happiness and sadness and love and hate coil about us, a constant battle of our wills and our conscious and unconscious states, affecting our dreams, aspirations, the decisions we make or don't, the actions and opportunities we take or let go. We make our excuses, justifying ourselves, the situation, our good luck or our misfortune, always the serpents duelling within, sometimes tightening their grip, sometimes loosening it, an eternal battle within the cycle of our lives and the vast cauldron of the universal forces.

But the duelling serpents are so much more, signifying the unity of the physical and the spirit of life. I was talking recently with my friend Bob Trubshaw, exploring the concept of the ancestral soul being held within the very bones of our bodies. We discussed the 'bone spirit' as representing the strength, wisdom and hidden knowledge, which in our modern day includes our understanding of the ancestral DNA, that helps to shape the physical and practical attributes carried forward from those who came before.

We also discussed soul of 'breath-spirit', the serpent, which is individual to us. This serpent represents our uniqueness and our consciousness, our life source and our personal spark of life. It is independent of the other ancestral serpent that is the Bone Spirit and yet forever entwined with it during life and only freed upon death. I think of them as the 'serpents of self' holding the hidden wisdom of heritage, culture, existence and stability and the life source of being. The soul of the bone spirit is the earth energies of the past and present as well as the potential for the future within the bones of our bodies and the ancestral DNA holding us within the vessel or body, supporting and working in partnership with the soul of breath spirit, the serpent of liminality, of consciousness and unconsciousness, of ideas, dreams and aspirations, of personality and intellect. Together coiling and spiralling around each other they strive for balance and equilibrium ensuring that the journey of life, death and rebirth continues.

We are creatures of habit, persuasion, selfishness, addictions, ego, fear and cruelty to ourselves or others. Feel the serpent's coils tighten and restrict. See it move swiftly, darting out of nowhere, sinking its fangs into your unsuspecting flesh. Feel the poison as it takes hold, as you lose control and consciousness. You are immobilised, mesmerised and held in its power…

But are we not also the creatures of invention, communication, inspiration, intellect, creativity, humour, laughter and love, not to mention generosity and of immense beauty? Feel this serpent coil and allow it to shed its skin when the need arises. Allowing time and space for the act of shedding leads to growth and renewal and allows transformation. Nothing is static, everything changes, everything moves. This is the nature of the serpent.

Know that both serpents are required to sustain us, they are essential to our existence. Journeying with them helps to find balance, allow the serpents to coil about us, within us and around each other in harmony and with equilibrium.

Lugus and Mercury
The Cave of the Duelling Serpents is perhaps one of the most outwardly influential energies that can affect us. It influences how we choose to engage with our lives and the outside world. Planetary wise, it is linked to Mercury which represents communication and connection. He is the god of commerce, travel, thievery and guide to all dead souls, the morning star and the evening star, messenger of the gods, lover of music and trickster. His symbol is the Caduceus, a staff with entwined serpents upon it and he has silver wings upon his shoes. Fast, fast, fast with sometimes extremes of behaviour and temperament; a lover of music and an accomplished musician, which he uses for both good

and bad. Mercury is apparently a god with no thought of others should there be something he wants, using his charms and talents to wriggle his way out of trouble.

To our ancestors, according to Julius Caesar, the god Mercury (Greek Hermes) was known as Lugus or Lleu Llaw Gryffes, one of the earliest known Brythonic Gods. In later times Odin and Loki were thought to have been influenced in their traits by Lugus or Mercury. Whatever the truth, his attributes, energies and importance was not restricted to one land or one people and as the millennia have passed we can argue that his influence and relevance has strengthened and become dominant.

It has been suggested to me by several people that in Britain, down the centuries, Lugus was split into a triad, and it is possible that he was latterly recognised as Esus, Taitatis and Taranus. I don't know how true this is but it is an interesting thought and I believe that there are statues or depictions of Lugus having three heads. Perhaps one out of the three personalities is now in charge? Perhaps we need to re-balance all three aspects?

In the modern era, I see mercurial or Lugus energy everywhere. The pace we live our lives, the fact that everything is up for grabs in a technological playground with information bombarded at us from every direction, it feels sometimes as though nothing is inaccessible any more, regardless of to whom it belongs or if we have worked for it or not. There seems to be a definite lackadaisical attitude regarding issues of privacy and little thought given to the relevance, need and accuracy of information. There are moral arguments as to whether we should have access to certain types of information at all. How can this help us? This is something I often struggle with. Where is our incentive to do things for ourselves, to take risks to learn? Am I just being an old cynic? Probably. Personally I am an advocate of freedom of information and free speech but I feel the points raised above are worthy of thought and consideration.

Go to the extreme, to excess and carry on until morning and

beyond appears to be the modern ethos of life. Addiction, dependency and control along with innovation, knowledge, progression and enlightenment are some of the predominant undercurrents of our world. With society wrapped in its security blanket of internet, television, mobile phones and in the mammoth technological progress that has been made of the last 50 years (and especially over the last 20 years) I ask myself are we children let lose in a sweet shop with no supervision and totally unaware of the dangers and harm that we are doing to ourselves by living on a continual diet of sugar and fat? I wonder sometimes if we have lost the ability to press the off button, to say no more and to just be still, quiet for a while so that we take stock and have the time, energy and space to move forward at a natural pace.

Interestingly, I looked up the etymology of Lugus because he represents a British god and thus a sacred energy for these lands and the people who live upon it, and this is what I found:

Lugus- derived from various Proto-Indo-European roots:

1: *Leug* meaning 'black'
2: *Leug* meaning 'to break'
3: *Leug* meaning 'to swear an oath'
4: *Plugo* or *Plu* meaning in Cymric 'feather'[1]

It occurred to me in each of those meanings there can be a plethora of interpretations both good and bad, some of which we have already discussed, which all could be applied to today's society and the individuals and communities that live within that society, but if we look specifically, can we not direct this at ourselves and our own lives?

Mercury/Lugas is also the god associated with beauty, creativity and all the arts, communication and potential, and there can be no

---

1   www.etymonline.com   and www.celtnet.org.uk

denying that all of these things exist in abundance upon this small but perfectly shaped planet of ours.

Perhaps we sometimes need to remember that this god's energy is not concerned with right and wrong, good or bad. Instead it is an essential part of living, of communicating, identifying with, of doing and being. However, what we chose to do and how we chose to do it is, ultimately, our own personal or collective human responsibility.

Time Out

Here am I talking about the excesses of today's society, talking about balance and the quality of life when typing away on my computer, mobile phone just to my side, hand held landline phone next to it, printer switched on ready and waiting and of course the television is never far away and again ready to dominate the living space once it is switched on, and the car, let's not forget the car which tells me daily I don't need my legs for walking anymore. Can I, or should I be, so reliant upon these items? What if I turned them all off and put them away, say for a week or maybe a month, how easy would it be to carry on in today's world? Would I be making life difficult for myself or would I be redressing a balance, freeing me up to other more stimulating and enriching things?

To be inaccessible for a period of time, to have to make the effort to visit, write, have conversations, debates, to entertain myself instead of being hypnotised and brainwashed in front of a square rectangle box…oh, the possibilities begin to dawn. Dinner parties, reading, time to sit and chat face to face, time to try out new activities and hobbies, time to listen to the world around me, to take walks and explore, time to just be still and silent, to rest and recharge.

Have we lost the ability to take time out, to be unobtainable and not constantly on call, linked by hundreds if not thousands of invisible unbiblical cords to all that modern society has to offer, for good and for bad and without prejudice and without balance?

So let's try it out, turn it all off, try a day, perhaps two, or maybe you feel you can give a week or a month to this exercise. Can this become something that becomes part of our routine that once a month or every other month, we give ourselves a break and do as we were told as children 'go and do something less boring instead'.

The Ritual of Being
Walking through the woods with twigs snapping underfoot, the smell of slightly damp, mossy earth lingers in the breeze wrapping me in its invisible cloak of security. As the light begins to fall away up through the wild honeysuckle, elder and demanding bracken, I continue my walk, weaving my path through the beech, holly and hazel until, at last, the majesty of the oak grove stands before me.

Thrice around the boundary walked, elemental forces called and welcomed, intent and purpose spoken aloud, energy thumping and drumming, rising, rising reaching out and penetrating all.

Spirit of place and ancestors honoured. Energy rising again, cone of power emanating, inspiration flowing, dancing and singing I spiral in and out, round and around. The veil is thin, magical forces hear the call, sense the need and understand the intent.

As darkness once again comes and you close your tired eyes, the ritual of the day finely comes to a close. All thoughts of the day that has been fade slowly and the ritual of rest, dreams and nightmares begins.

Our individual ritual of being, a labyrinth of twists and turns as unique as we are and as necessary as every breath we take is an instinctual and a natural part of who and what we are. For the most part it passes us by unnoticed, accepted by us as just participating in the day to day routine of living and yet, by its very definition, the ritual of being who and what we are shapes our lives and our understanding of our place within the cycle of all things.

The unending cycle of life of the duelling serpents is the greatest ritual that we will ever participate in. Everything we do is a ritual born out of the motivation of needs which are dictated by survival or by feelings of inadequacy and defence driving us until a particular need is fulfilled or denied. Ritual is the manifestation of our inherent need for personal growth, survival and empowerment. We need the good things in life, the treats and luxuries that can provide quality of life, but be aware that nothing is gained without sacrifice and too much of a good thing is never good. Striving for balance in what can often feel like a very unbalanced world is perhaps what life is all about: balance, harmony and quality of life. Therein lies the mystery - what represents quality of life for you?

JOURNEYING INTO THE CAVE OF THE DUELLING SERPENTS

Part 1: The Journey
(Play back Part 1 taken from Chapter 1, or read out the transcript to assist you as you journey.)

As your prepare for you journey into the Cave of the Duelling Serpents, think about the dualities in your life, your loves and hates, your obsessions, good or bad. Remember this is not about being judgemental nor is it about denial, instead this is a place of personal identity, of colour, shapes and sounds. The Duelling Serpents are not energies that are good or bad, they are what they are and their gifts give you a voice, expression and choice. How you use these energies is down to you, remember this is about personal responsibility and balance.

Part 2: Into the Caves
When you reach your cave, note your surroundings. How does this place make you feel? What or who can you see and how is your cave furnished, if at all?

You can say whatever you want in this place, you can be however you want to be and you can make whatever changes you want or feel you need, because within this cave the focus can only be about you.

Don't fear your needs, wants, cravings or addictions, in whatever manner they manifest. Don't fear change, adjustment, inclusion or exclusion, just understand and know it is okay, nothing is static and these things can be developed, stopped, changed moved on, whatever is needed and it is your choice and your responsibility because it is your life.

We are all different and we are multifaceted with light and dark sides and that is okay; it is what is required in order to be alive. The skill is to balance all sides of ourselves or at least know when enough is enough and when it is time to realign ourselves with our internal scales.

Part 3: The Return and Awakening
Use the transcript provided in Chapter 1. Awaken from your journey happy and refreshed.

THE BREATH OF BONE AND SPIRIT OF BREATH TALISMAN
This is such a personal exercise that you may feel the need to take time out to think about exactly what the Breath of Bone and Spirit of Breath represent in your own life, for these are the Duelling Serpents that coil within and without, holding you and nurturing you in whatever way that manifests for you. Perhaps meditate on what it is you want the talisman to represent. Do you need balance in a particular area of your life? Do you need to decide if there are issues of too much or not enough within your life? What are you trying to achieve by balancing your internal serpents and what symbolism are you going to use?

I cannot provide step by step instruction on what you should or shouldn't do in the making of your talisman because it is so personal and must be representative of you and your intent. However, there are many forms that a talisman can take and no limits on what it can be made from be it clay, metal, jewellery of some kind, or wood. The method and the materials you use will be about you, your intent and whatever symbolism you decide upon. This really is about you and your personal choice.

In your deliberations think about the contents of the chapter you have just read and how it resonates with you. You may feel empathy with all or some of what I have said, but then again some things may not resonate with you which again is normal but may have raised questions within you. If this is so then take these thoughts on your journey into the Cave of Duelling Serpents and seek further answers and resolutions.

Remember this is about you and nobody else. This is your journey, your life and your web and nobody but you is responsible for it.

Wild Women

Forever fighting, we march to the drum,
The life-giving warriors,
Not afraid when death duly comes,
Misunderstood mysteries wrapped tightly around us,
A cloak of fear,
But wait and judge us not,
First let your eyes truly clear.

Proud and strong, we battle on and on,
Wild women all,
Listen and hear our song,
Maiden, Mother, Crone,
Our call is as one,
Ensuring for all time
There's a future for those yet to come.

Chapter 6
THE CAVE OF THE ETERNAL WARRIORS

"I am fighting as an ordinary person for my freedom, my bruised body and my out raged daughters...Consider how many of you are fighting ...and why. Then you will win this battle, or perish. That is what I, a Woman, plan to do!"
Boudicca (60 CE) as cited in *Eve's Revenge* 1994 Tama Starr, also cited in *Boudica's Speeches in Tacitus and Dio* by Eric Adler published in 'Project Muse, Scholarly Journals Online' 2008

The pregnant woman, so beautiful, so full of anticipation out in the light of the blazing sun with all her potential growing, nurtured and loved. See her for the radiance that she throws about her, her beauty maturing, voluptuous and curvaceous. She is whole, flowering gracefully as her young are gathered, her ideas, her children, her intent and her dreams manifested, for she is the Mother.

Anxiety and excitement, the wonderment of life growing within, it is worth all the pain, blood and excrement, worth the sacrifice. The agony of ripped and torn skin is all forgotten as life takes its first breath and utters its first cry. Such joy, tears of pure love and achievement. The swelling of the woman recedes as the Mother is now born along with the child whose cord is cut for the first time.

This is also the song of the midwife, she who brings things into being, enabling the song of the mother to fill the air as she gives birth. The God energy is splendid at this time, his canopy of green offering the mother and her children shade. At the peak of his power the Mother is content to let her Lord have his time, for she knows it is for the benefit of all, and as time passes her strength, knowledge and power begins its ascent, but she is in no hurry; her time will come as surely as night follows day.

Suckling woman, nurturing and loving Mother, she who knows the cycle of things to come and yet still she embraces the opportunities and struggles to establish herself. Finally when all is done, then and only then will she allow herself to bask in the luxury of her success. See her in all things, in all that is in full bloom, in the richness of the harvest, in the achievement of your endeavours and know and feel her in the lushness of nature because in truth we are part of it, part of her.

In the home of the Mother all things are brought to fruition, healthy and full of vitality, strong and courageous; her pride in all things is without question. Mistake not her tears when her young leave the nest, she understands the natural order, but don't underestimate the wrench, for this pulls from the deepest recesses. For mother and child this is the second cutting of the cord.

This is not the end, for there is still the anticipation of one more cut to come, and like any mother she knows the third cut will be just as painful if not more so, but there is still time, for this cut will be made at the end when she is no more. This is the time of endings and new beginnings as the Mother makes her solitary journey, descending into darkness, stepping through the gates of Annwn. In the darkness, all consuming, she takes her rest, prepares and focuses on rejuvenation until it is her time to come again, when the wheel has turned and those that she has given birth to will, in turn, give birth themselves.

In the summer of life, the full moon bright and shiny, a warm glow around the Mother radiates. Her nest is built and her children thriving. Now she is strong in purpose, a most fearless warrioress in protection of those she loves. Hearth and home is her stronghold, she is the healer, the teacher, and she is fulfilled. See her confidence grow as she is seen for her value and worth. Hear her joy and laughter floating on a warm gentle breeze. She is community, she is the harvest and she is the song of achievement. Beautiful and voluptuous, round and soft, inviting, with her mead horn flowing over for she is the rain that nourishes and feeds, the she-wolf that protects her family, the bear that stands strong and unrepentant in her natural state of being.

The crops and bounty of the land are ripening; all is well, prosperity and creativity in practice that is the manifestation of the Awen in all that is life. The heady scents of meadowsweet, honeysuckle, rose and evening primrose mingle with the night scented stock and sweet bryony. All are her natural perfumes, she stimulates our senses, allowing us to remember that we are connected, basking in the memories of summers past and summers yet to come. Gently her breeze floats across the craggy brook, through the trees and woodlands, through the fields and meadows, through the gardens, open doors and windows and finally through us, wrapping her arms lovingly around and caressing, comforting us as only a mother can.

The sacred Mother Goddess, eternal in her magic, she is the dance and the spirit of summer, with the gentle rise and fall of her breasts seen in the hills and mountains and the curves of her body shaping the land. The wisdom and knowledge she holds is nurturing and protecting, her eternal sacrifice ensuring all have the opportunity to attain their full potential.

She is the weaver, her web of destiny finely spun. Bright and shiny she is the huntress, provider and protector. Let no one approach her young uninvited, let no one threaten her sanctuary. She knows her worth for she is majestic, in full bloom, radiant in her accomplishments, in her security. Queen of her own domain, her cauldron of creativity over flowing, resplendent in her own majesty watching her children grow and marvelling in their potential and gifts, her labour is done and her children out in the world.

The fruits of the hedgerow and orchards are beginning to ripen, the bee is heavy with pollen and life is good. The Mother keeps house well and none shall go without for her larder is full. Proud huntress, warrior and protector, no sacrifice is too small. Unforgiving and relentless should her loved ones be at risk of harm or damage. Beware her wrath if undermined, beware her vengeance should her will be thwarted, and know that her retaliation will be swift, deadly and just.

Bountiful lady, sword mother, corn mother, lady of the orchard, weaver of fate, she of the full moon, her potential fulfilled complete and whole. Spider mother dedicated to the needs of others. She can wear herself out with her need to make things right as she fears her young will feel stifled if not given free expression. Indulgent and patient the Great Mother hears all, sees all, nothing is missed and much, at times, will be said.

She is noble in her intent, full of integrity in deed but arrogant in her endeavours, for is not mother always right? She understands, even if those about her don't, that her primary role is to feed and nurture her children so that they may grow. The mother, who is an important primary facet of the Eternal Warrior, sees her own and others' paths clearly and always knows what is best. She is generous with her time and gives her advice freely and is happy to guide and provide options. A mother's love to hold us and to help us make sense of the world around us is beyond price, and yet can be overwhelming. She is the one who sets the boundaries which others will kick against.

She is the teacher, healer, sister, daughter, wife and lover. She is all thing to all people, a natural chameleon, adaptable, multi-tasking, accommodating, always available and her time often not her own. Silently she is often screaming inside for her lost independence because she has forgotten who she is, believing - even knowing - that there is more to life and yet little time to find it. Life's tapestry can be so complex that it is difficult for us to attempt to read the pattern, let alone follow it.

When we feel overwhelmed, or feel that the task in front of us is far above our capabilities we are telling ourselves that we are bound to fail. We have convinced ourselves that we will fail so there is a very good chance that this will result in us failing to recognise that our personal tapestry can be delicate and but at the same time vibrant and strong. By recognising the incorporation of your individual design, your personal pattern, with the thickness and type of thread that you have chosen to use, you will see that what has been created is a stunning and beautiful weave, all strands of the threads intertwined and stitched in their rightful place so that when standing from afar the whole picture is revealed.

Like all weaves, the designs can be changed and can be as simple or as complicated as you choose, but the beauty of who you are remains within the individuality of the weave. Our life journey is our greatest individual spell of intent and it is the Sacred Mother that shows us how to thread the needle and where the best threads can be found. *"We all come from the Goddess and to her we shall return"* is a popular chant that is sung all over the world, not one of my favourites but nonetheless it is sung as an acknowledgement of the Great Mother Goddess.

Spirit of the Warrior

Know me as I am floating high over the land, the wind whipping my face with my hair flying freely out behind me. Below the hills, rivers and fields merge into greens and blues, feeding my spirit. My wings spread with ease, my feathers keeping me warm. I am free, as free as the air I breathe, there are no limitations, there is nothing to stand in my way, I can go wherever I want to for I manifest my own reality and I am in my natural state of being.

Hit the drum and stamp our feet in rhythm and let our voices be heard as we call to the spirits within and without to join us, to fuel the rise in energy.

We dance our rites around the trees and fires, release, then draw in, release then breathe in. The energy, the weave, the Awen, the inspiration manifested, setting our intent; we are passionate, walking our truth, finding our path, we are shown the way.

We are magnificent, we are warriors, strong willed, dedicated in our task, basking in the lunar and solar energies. We, with courage, step into our power, radiating the truth of who we are, not afraid, not ashamed, we are truly whole, Eternal Warriors, ready, waiting and full of life.

All around the greenwood is in full bloom, alive and vibrant, protecting and a teaching parent. The elemental spirits dance and laugh, they are the keepers of the deepest magic, ages old knowledge, but believe, no *know,* that it is there, that they are there, waiting for us to join with them for they understand that we are part of them as they are part of us. It is an unspoken sadness, our disconnectedness that blinds us to what is obvious, all around and a universal truth.

Hear the drum of the eternal heartbeat that connects us all back to the beginning of all things. Spinning and spiralling towards the centre of everything, a personal labyrinth intrinsic to the song of self, but one that takes us all, eventually, to the centre of its pathways, the place of stillness, of introspection, of knowing of who and what we are. We are opened up to the possibilities, to anticipation and to the inner truth of who and what we truly are.

This is not a quick route for this is our life journey and the labyrinth will twist and turn, sometimes leading us down blind alleys but there is only one path within any labyrinth that leads to the centre and our task is to find that way with as few detours as we are able. Of course some detours are necessary and a part of our learning curve; it is how we progress, understanding what works for us and what does not. However, perhaps if we were not so afraid to be intuitive, listen to ourselves and of take personal responsibility, it would be a more enjoyable ride?

I am child of my Mother,
Mother of my child,
I am a bridge between
Yesterday and tomorrow.
Indigo Pangea (2004 WeMoon Diary)

Finding the Internal Warrior

When we talk of the Eternal Warrior aspect of the sacred feminine are we specific in our meaning? Are we stating that those of us who do not have children are not included in this phase of life, in this manifestation of the Goddess? Of course not, this is about a time in our personal cycle when we are bright and shiny, in full bloom and in our prime.

In the early days we are finding our path, sowing the seeds of intent for the direction our lives will take. We are nest building, setting up hearth and home, finding out what our strengths and weaknesses are. We strive to do well, to be recognised and we expect the rewards of hard work. During this time we increase our social network, establish ourselves within the community that we feel best suits us and that we identify with.

We are the trendsetters, the rule makers and the law givers. We are the listening ear, the shoulder to cry on and we open up our arms and embrace those around us and those in need. We are full of energy in the early days, just like nature around us we shine, we bloom, we are in full colour and we are awesome in our beauty and achievements. These are all the qualities of the Eternal Warrior as the Eternal Warrior is our dedication, determination, courage and pride, how we conduct ourselves with honour and compassion. All of these qualities enable us to cope and face the good times and the hardships and tragedies that life throws at us. The Eternal Warrior understands the use of energy, just as our ancestors understood the concept of going into battle knowing the likelihood was that they would not return, and this energy enables us to do that which is normally outside of our day to day existence; it is the core of our survival instincts, it is the fire within the passion and the desire to succeed, overcome and thrive.

I believe that our ancestors understood this concept and rewarded with great generosity those who showed and demonstrated talent, courage, strength, creativity, honour and integrity. The torc is a symbol of an individual's, or even a tribe's, wealth, importance and status and was worn with pride for deeds done and would have been respected by others.

It is a sad reflection on craft/Druidry and society today that such a display of openly wearing or the giving of the torc, whether actually or metaphorically, would be viewed by many as boastful and egotistical behaviour; we appear to be resentful of acknowledging another's achievements.

I wear my torc as a reminder of who and what I am. It is a personal statement of intent, a show of my personal strength, courage and power. It is also a display of my status, my wealth and my worth. It is a promise made between me and my Gods not to throw away my torc again, however well intended. My torc is a gift from my Gods in recognition of lessons learned and a return to my inner self, acknowledging my worth, my gifts, my intent and my commitment. That was a big admission to make and it has been a difficult journey to get to this place and I still have a way to go.

When we are in the phase of life we attribute to the Mother aspect of the Goddess, life is full in many different ways. We might be forging ahead with our careers, socialising and partying, dealing with hearth and home as well as raising our children, if we have any, managing ever spiralling costs of living whilst trying to maintain the general equilibrium around us. Life is noisy, rushed, tiring and often hard work and yet there is an energy that enables us to face each day with gusto, to multi-task and split ourselves in order to fulfil everyone's requirements.

The rituals and the magic of the Mother aspect of the sacred feminine fill our everyday lives, from giving birth and naming our children to the day to day personal rituals of bathing, dressing and putting on our makeup, rituals of healing and nurturing, cooking and feeding and going to work. She shows herself in whatever capacity is relevant at that time. Of course there is also the ritual altar that is our home which by its very nature is filled with meaning, purpose and intent and is a statement of who we are which conveys, in part, this message to others.

Everything we do within our daily routine has intent of one form or another and can be viewed as the practical ritulisation of living. In my home I have actual altars in various parts of the house and garden and they change and grow depending on the time of year, how I am feeling, my intent and my need.

But what is the nature of the Sacred Mother and what are her magical rituals? We who nurture, nourish and give birth, we who are the healers, the lovers, the wives, sisters, mothers and daughters, what are our experiences and how can we implement our craft into sacred ritual, manifesting the magic of our intent? I cannot speak for others in this and you may or may not resonate with what I have chosen to share within this chapter.

Often we don't have time to think about ourselves, the impact our punishing regimes places on us emotionally, physically and practically. We often set ourselves up, expect ourselves to be able to cope, to be all things to all people. Where is the off button and the enough all ready button? I'm still looking for mine. So what's the magical and craft angle in all this? It concerns the energy exchange, the implementation of energy in everyday life, making things happen, the undying enthusiasm, inspiration and creativity that keeps everyday life and us, within it, afloat.

I love the altars that I have in the house because they are a reflection of where I am in my life. They are a focus that enables me to cope and re-affirm my intent, an outward expression what I am hoping to achieve, what I no longer want or am no longer prepared to put up with. Of course the intent and focus should not be just about the taking, but also about the giving of yourself. A little piece of you, of what you represent, the manifestation of magic is, as always, about sacrifice, be that of your time, an object of value and or even your blood. The importance of this lies in the connection energetically that it represents. It is your essence, your commitment, your focus, and it is your significator, and I use the term significator here specifically as a focal point that represents you within the ritual and the magic of intent that you are creating. How you look after your altar and what has been incorporated on it is another reflection of how you feel and how you view yourself. On many levels, an altar is an extension of you with things that have meaning and represent hopes, fears, aspirations, dreams and experiences. It is a statement to the Gods and the world around you that communicates something about you and your needs, and altars should be taken seriously in their construction and use.

In 1997 I had my hysterectomy. Unbelievably I was told that I might feel less of a woman and that my then husband might also view me as not being a 'proper women' anymore. The latter was sadly true, hence the reason why he is now my ex-husband. However, it was a very hard time; my body changed completely due to the illness and I didn't recognise myself in the mirror. After the operation one of the things I did was to make a Goddess out of clay. Her middle was hollow making a cave so that I could place a candle within to remind me that the light within me still burned, and that physically and energetically nothing had changed to make me any less a woman.

I had a very dear friend back then who was a ceramicist and she helped me with this process, firing and glazing my Lady in beautiful blues. My Goddess is still with me and she travels with me as part of my mobile altar where ever I go. She is an important reminder of a time of pain, of fighting for life and of not giving up. She epitomises my determination and my refusal to accept other people's expectations.

Sadly, in 2007 I needed further treatment and a further operation. I hadn't experienced bleeding from my vagina for over ten years and then I did. It was a shock since I don't have a womb. I had not worn sanitary towels or even thought about it. Towels with wings, how novel, and ones that are unbleached, about time too and bio-degradable, will wonders never cease! I obviously couldn't use my moon-cup and no longer had any of my washable towels and I couldn't find any to buy either. Had the bleeding continued I would have made myself some like

I used to, but for nearly two months I was transported back in time and it gave me an opportunity to collect my blood and I was able to anoint my Goddess with it. I acknowledge this was not blood from my womb but my cervix (or what was left of my cervix) instead. Nevertheless, it is the intent that is critical and my ritual reinforced my intent to treat myself with more kindness, regardless of the bits no longer physically part of me and to know that energetically I am intact.

It sounds so easy doesn't it? It wasn't. I have to be honest I have struggled with this for years, but I am getting there and maybe that's the point. I do view myself differently these days and my personal rituals reflect that. I do not feel the need to be ever compliant, ever available, forever trying to be somebody who fits in with others' sensitivities and needs. That sounds selfish but that is not my intent. Those about me now love me for me, not because I look after them, take responsibility for their lives, or because I look good on their arms like the stereotype of women in the media or a Stepford wife.

In times of hardship and crisis we tend to give more of ourselves, our energy is stretched and put under pressure. We are tested on all levels but even then we often ignore our inner senses. There are times in our lives when we struggle, financially, emotionally, practically or physically. Our energy will be low and fragmented, yet we are still able to maintain concern for others, perhaps because we cannot face our own issues and it is easier to direct our attention in another direction until we reach that critical mass point when we breakdown or shut down all together.

On one level we can view this as an amazing time of transformation, personal growth and inspiration. It doesn't necessarily feel like this at the time, but there is truth in the saying 'out of chaos comes order' and we learn so much about ourselves and about our own needs at such moments. We redefine our boundaries, look differently at those around us and they will look at us in a different light; relationships are reaffirmed and forged or lost and broken.

However, if we look at this from the aspect of the Mother

Goddess, it is perhaps akin to the intense pain and the unstoppable release of control during labour and yet with that hidden knowledge within us, we realise that the end result is worth the struggle. To fight against the natural tide only makes the labour harder, longer and more painful.

I have never found letting go easy. I have never liked giving up personal control and I have made life harder than it needed to be at certain points. However, I have no regrets because I did what I did and made the choices that I made in good faith and hindsight is a wonderful thing. My biggest criticism of myself is that in the past I thought it was 'my job' to make everything better and everything ok for everyone else. I took responsibility in situations that was not mine to take and in the end found myself surrounded by needy and dysfunctional individuals and that, in the end, included me. I crashed, I could not cope but my boundaries were set to such a degree that I couldn't see that like attracts like and it was ultimately my responsibility to change the energy, including my energy, changing my direction and allowing others to do the same. Our energy will mirror how we see ourselves and how we see the world. I was able to acknowledge that in some relationships our time together was now at an end, though I might have been dragged kicking and screaming to that point.

It is interesting that the Gods try to guide us, putting us in situations and providing us with opportunities, yet how many times do we miss the boat, ignore what we feel and see, failing to act in time or failing to act at all? I have always found that if we stray too far from the path the Gods have a way of ensuring that we are brought to a grinding halt until we open our eyes and ears.

Some people call this the 'dark night of the soul' when we question everything and everyone. The truth is we do eventually emerge with a change of direction, re-defined boundaries and with clarity about who and what we are. Of course not everyone around you will like the changes, not everyone will understand and that, I know from personal experience, is very hard and painful.

The Great Universal Mother gives life but also takes it.. She lets things run their natural course regardless of how long or how short that is. She understands the cycle of all things and the roles that are played out. As the Goddess manifest, we too face this challenge. Most of us, at different points in our lives, must actually let loved ones go, from children leaving the nest, relationships breaking down and those we love passing away. Death is hard, especially the death of a child. Many of us may experience miscarriage as a natural occurrence, insomuch as part of us is not prepared or the pregnancy is not viable. Regardless, the loss for many is unbearably acute as we focus on the loss of our unborn children and the lost potential of motherhood. We may have to cope with feelings of inadequacy and worse still, because our babies did not survive it is hard to grieve openly and to acknowledge this loss and the feelings that can engulf us.

The Eternal Mother, the Sword Mother, she who never gives up regardless of the odds, knows when to strike and when to retreat. She keeps us alive, she allows us to overcome our challenges and the capacity to heal within, to heal others and eventually to let go of those things, feelings and people who are detrimental to our wellbeing. This aspect of the Goddess has been at the fore of who I am for most of my life. She has given me the courage and the strength to face adversities in my life, but she has also given me the insight and optimism to never give up my dreams.

I was very young, 22 years old, when my daughter Charlotte died, a week before her second birthday. I cannot in all honesty tell you that I went straight to my altar and drew strength from my Gods, nor was I particularly, at that point, feeling supported by my Gods. In fact, I hated them, which was a natural response under the circumstances. Due to Charlotte's illness, my craft, in terms of practicing ritual and study, had gone out of the window. It was not my primary concern. However, you cannot change the core of who you are and I am my craft and vice versa. I know no other way and I did call on the Sword Mother to help me. The Eternal Warrior within never gave up hope but in the end I understood that I had to let Charlotte go. It may sound strange, but Charlotte herself let me know when that time had come.

I cannot put into words how my life shattered into tiny fragments or describe the desolation, physical pain or the screaming agony that tore every fibre of my being apart. I cannot express the anger, guilt and the relief, relief that my beautiful child was no longer suffering and in so much pain, relief that I no longer had to watch that suffering and wait for the day that she would be taken from me. I felt desolate and destroyed; my life had no meaning, the agonising screams that had come from Charlotte as she fought for life as her little heart gave out and her lungs filled with blood were the only sounds I could hear... I was deafened by them. Nothing would or could be the same again and nothing made sense in my life any more. When she died, part of me died with her. Her blood was my blood, her bones were made from my bones and I was totally and utterly powerless as she lay there dying in such pain; all I could do was hold her and call to all that I held sacred that she didn't suffer any more.

I was two months pregnant with my second daughter, Lucci, when Charlotte died. I was told not to grieve too much and that I needed to pull myself together.

"Do you want to kill this baby as well?" were the kind and understanding words of a local GP. "Although," he said, "I really do not see the problem here. It's not as if you aren't young enough to have another one is it?" What can I say? I wasn't as mellow as I am now. The Sword Mother raged through my veins and the doctor never saw the door open as I 'escorted' him off the premises.

Charlotte has been dead for over twenty years and she now resides in the house of my ancestors. She is loved by us all and on the anniversary of her death, the 1ˢᵗ March, and on her birthday the 12ᵗʰ March, she is remembered by all the family. The altar is hers and I honour her as my daughter, for her courage and amazing bravery and for the gifts that she left me in memories and the things I learned and the people I met as a result of her, but more importantly for the gift that was her, Charlotte my daughter. It is truly an honour to be her mother, because regardless of where she now resides, whether it is in this world or through the gates of Annwn, I am still her mother and she is still my child and that will never change.

Does it get easier as the years fall away? No. Never. In fact it gets harder, harder to remember every detail, harder sometimes to believe that she was actually here, harder not to feel cheated.

I could not carry out any passing-over and death rites for Charlotte's funeral as her father and his family are Christians. However, when she lay in the chapel of rest I went to see her with my grandma. We blessed her and covered her in beautiful flowers. We placed rosebuds in her hair, we placed spring flowers, primrose and cowslip, around her head and then we placed freesias, carnations and more roses all over her until she was swaddled in a blanket of the sweetest smelling flowers. She looked so beautiful, dreaming in an eternal sleep.

She was buried with so many of her favourite things, books, dolls and photos of me and her dad, that there was hardly any room for her. My friend's son Matthew, who was Charlotte's best friend, wrote her a story that we placed in the coffin with her for, in his words, "this is so my Larlot (that's what her called her) will have something to read so she won't get bored on her journey to live in the stars". What can you say to that?

In 2008, when Charlotte would have celebrated her 21st birthday, I felt I needed to perform a ritual of reconnection and remembrance but more importantly an acknowledgement and a release (see Chapter 8). It was empowering and felt so right and healing. It has taken me twenty years to get to this point but I see her beauty and innocence in much around me. I have always drawn on her strength and courage and part of my ritual was reaffirming the bonds that join us as mother and daughter. Blood of my blood, bone of my bone, she is part of me as I am part who she was. This cannot change because we are part of the same ancestral line stretching behind me, and so the part of me that is part of her walks that path with her, for that is always the truth for any parent and their child. Of course, usually we expect them to take us into the future, not to become part of our past.

The Sword Mother became an important aspect to me over the subsequent years, and over and over again I called upon her, on her wisdom, strength and courage. The danger is becoming too defensive, too rigid in your boundaries and personal protections which can be born out of an acute need for self preservation. I think I am being honest when I say that this is certainly what happened to me. The Sword Mother claimed me totally, appropriately for the most part but not so when she becomes a constant companion. It is a hard one to admit to, let alone change, but I have moved on and as they say 'with age should come wisdom' and I am more at ease with who I am and certainly more confident where my craft is concerned. Not that I don't intend to grow old disgracefully mind you; it's a family legacy. Bless you grandma.

The Eternal Warrior is with us through the good and the bad times. She is our instinct, she is our eternal fire and even on rainy days when the fire is reduced to a smoulder we would do well to remember that it never truly goes out. I have realised as I've got older that the trick is to work with this aspect of the sacred feminine, to respect and honour her within and without, and also to remember to balance this part of myself and allow movement and development. This allows the Eternal Warrior to acquire new skills whilst continuing to develop existing ones. The Eternal Warrior is the truth and the strength of our spirits and it is this that lets us know we are truly alive. The Eternal Warrior determines how we cope, how we respond to situations and interact with those around us; she is our courage and determination. She enables us to move forward and follow our paths singing the song of self and of the truth that is our lives.

When we look at our lives and assess the experiences, how do we see ourselves? Do we feel regret? Do we wish we had done things differently? Do we believe that we had little or no control over events and that the consequences have been lost dreams, feelings of inadequacy and low self esteem? All of us could probably answer 'yes' at some point in our lives.

I remember an exercise I was asked to do when I was at university, identifying my strengths and weaknesses. I had two pages full of faults and only a few lines of positives. We are good at underestimating and undermining ourselves and not recognising our own worth, talents or the undying warrior spirit that keeps us going when all else has crashed around our ears.

If we look back through history we can find that the magic and enchantment of the warrioress shines brightly down through the ages all the way back to the beginning. We find women being themselves, standing in their own power, often against great odds and in hostile environments. These women wove their magic and their craft and allowed the light to shine, embracing all that life threw at them, the good and very often the bad. We are no different from these women of history, we too have our truths and fight bravely in our own personal battles:

> So take up the banner
> Let your hair flow free
> Acknowledge the fire and the energy within
> Primal powers set forth in all its glory
> Rejoice in womankind and her eternal story

JOURNEYING INTO THE CAVE OF THE ETERNAL WARRIORS

Part 1: The Journey
(Play back Part 1 taken from Chapter 1, or read out the transcript to assist you as you journey.)

During your preparation to journey in to the Cave of the Eternal Warriors, allow yourself to think about all of the obstacles you have overcome at various times throughout your life. Perhaps there are still some obstacles that are drawing your attention and that are in need of addressing. That's ok, maybe that is the purpose of your cave and you need to galvanise and empower yourself so that you may act when you feel the time is right. The Cave of Eternal warriors may also be a place to remember, a place to recognise all that has been, what you have overcome or lost. Around the walls of the cave you may hang your shields of achievement, defence and loss, it matters not, because it will always remain a place of internal power, courage and strength from which you can draw whenever the need arises.

Part 2: Into the Caves

Imagine a spectacle of colour and symbols around the walls of your cave - the shields of protection, each with an image that depicts a time when it was used and needed. Maybe some are more battered and broken that others or maybe they are bright and shiny and unused. As you look about you, perhaps you can also see the discarded internal armour of defence, scattered about the cave or hanging up in various parts of the cave, maybe rusty but perhaps well oiled and shiny, over-used and now a little small for its owner. See swords, shields and spears, all of the tools a warrior might need. Think about the appropriateness of what is around you, what is inappropriate in your life, what has outgrown its usefulness and what is actually needed and should be used? Always remember it is what is relevant to you, but challenge yourself and most of all be honest, because if you aren't the only one affected will be you.

Part 3: The Return and Awakening

Use the transcript provided in Chapter 1. Return and awaken from your journey happy and refreshed.

THE RITUAL OF REMEMBRANCE AND RE-CONNECTION

This ritual was a personal experience and as such had a specific intent. For a long time I had felt very strongly that I needed to re-acknowledge my connection with my daughter Charlotte. This year she would have been 21 years old on March the 12th but I acutely felt the anger and pain that she had been dead for nineteen years on March 1st which overshadowed the joy that I had during her life. I needed to focus my pain in a constructive and healing way. On the day of Charlotte's birthday I retreated to my cabin in the heart of Swithland Woods where I performed the following ritual:

In the four directions, I lit four candles and in front of each candle I placed the following:

- In the north: I placed earth from the place of my birth and Charlotte's birth, representing the place of our ancestors and of the hearth and home we shared.
- In the east: I lit incense that I had made which represented the place of our dreams and memories.
- In the south: I placed a small fire dish with a lit fire which represented the place of love and the spark of life.
- In the west: I placed my cauldron filled with blessed spring water and this represented the place of healing of the flowing blood.

Sitting within the circle that I had created with the four directions, I cut a small amount of my hair and, along with a few precious strands of Charlotte's hair, I bound them together to make two small plaits. Within the plaits I placed rosemary for remembrance. I chanted the following as I wove the hair together:

I call to the Ancient Grandmothers of my blood,
Hear me and give me strength.

Once the weaving was finished I placed the plaits in the centre of the circle in front of me. Then I made a tiny poppet of clay that represented

Charlotte, chanting as I made it:

Child of spirit with all of nature's force
Hear me and give me strength.

My little clay poppet was then placed in the centre of the circle and I picked up both plaits and passed them through the four elements in the following way:

I call to the Ancient Grandmothers of my blood,
Hear me and give me strength.

With love and remembrance child born of my womb (the earth of our birth was sprinkled and rubbed into the plaits).

With love and remembrance Breath of my Dreams (the plaits were smudged with the incense).

With love and remembrance Spark of my Spirit (the plaits were passed through the flame of the fire).

With love and remembrance Blood of my Blood (the plaits were immersed in the blessed water of the cauldron).

I placed one of the plaits down by the side of the poppet and held the other one out in front of me. With a quick prick of my finger with a very sharp and sterilised needle, I drew blood allowing the drops to fall onto the plait. As I did this I called the following:

I call to you my child (Charlotte) and call you close as I walk between the worlds with you by my side. Know you are remembered. Know you are missed. Know that you are always loved.
    *A strengthening and a reminder of our eternal bond (*a few

drops of blood into the fire*), ancestors of my tribe and of my land, take the offering that I make and hold my child close in my stead. Together we are bound; this blood is your blood as it is mine.*

I then placed the plait into the flame of the fire and watched it burn. The remaining plait I smudged with the remaining blood and bound it around the little clay poppet, along with an owl and hawk feather, a tiny double-headed axe and primroses. I placed everything into a small leather pouch that I had made, securing it with a leather thong and wax.

It was an emotional ritual but so uplifting as well as strange as that might sound. I felt a sense of peace and release that I cannot remember ever feeling, certainly not concerning Charlotte and after all these long years it felt so right and so good.

In preparing for my rite I was also drawn to remember the three babies I had lost due to miscarriages. It was difficult because I have rarely allowed myself to think of them. I had not known them nor had I known their sex. I had never looked upon their tiny faces or cradled them in my arms and yet I could not deny that the pain and the loss were there. I also felt a real sense of guilt that as their mother I had never done anything to acknowledge them and claim them as my lost children.

I could not carry out an identical ritual to the one I had performed for Charlotte. However, I made three tiny clay poppets and, along with strands of my hair and black ribbon, I plaited a cord to bind around them. I then followed the same elemental call and blessing that I had for Charlotte, only slightly adapting the words. I sacrificed a bit more of my hair and a few more drops of blood to the fire calling to my ancestors as before. Then I wrapped them in silk and also placed them into a leather pouch along with owl and hawk feathers and spring flowers, cowslip and dried rose petals. Both pouches are kept with me when I am in ritual and at other times when I have a need, and both pouches are very precious to me.

Chapter 7
THE CAVE OF THE DREAMING GODDESS

There is a Goddess in me,
I am learning her dances by the dark of the moon,
Feet to moss,
Hand to bark,
Ear to wind,
Eye to Venus,
She awakens and sings
"Oh moon-dancing woman
Blessed Be."

I am she, reaching down into the very depths of who I am. My journey has taken many twists and turns, some of them hard and never-ending, some of them brief, fleeting experiences that have nonetheless helped to shape my life.

I am the mirror of my shadow side, the un-conforming and secret practice that can render me uncomfortable and sometimes embarrassed. I am the raging torrent that crashes unforgiving into the rocks and cliff face, I am the storm that screams its song so loudly that it drowns out all other noise, I am the volcano that erupts spewing forth hot molten lava not caring where it lands. But am I not also the gentleness of a summer breeze, the joy heard in a babbling stream, the innocence of a bright spring day, life giver and nurturer, comforter and lover? I am all of these things and more. I am complex, unrepentant and un-accepting of being anything other than what I am. In all my destructiveness, in all my beauty and creativity, I am the child that needs reassurance, love, strength and support. I need to feel safe with the freedom to explore and the amazement and excitement of achievement. I am the gemstone yet to be found buried within the ground, unspoilt, hidden, whose value is undeniable, holding all of my potential that is eternal and has yet to be realised, because I am 'She'.

The magical and hidden mysteries of women can be seen in every aspect of who we are from the way we are taught the facts of life, the way we express ourselves and live our lives to the legacy we pass on to the next generation.

Behind us is an ancestral line that is bright and vibrant, flowing back into the mists of time, those that went before us without whom we would not exist. All of our individual lines are as old as time and go back to the beginning of humankind. These are the roots of us as individuals, the tree of who and what we are; it is the strength of those roots that gives us our stability, our nourishment and that sense of being and belonging. We are the sum total of all who have been before and we remain part of the ancestors as they will always be part us, and this truth will never change. We too, one day, will take the rightful place that has already been reserved for us from the moment of our birth, a place that ensures that we will become part of that line and path which stretches back through the ages yet maintains its legacy firmly in the present, taking us into the future and those who are to come after.

Throughout the world the image of the Goddess can be seen everywhere, from the heights of Mount Olympus in Greece and the vast expanse that was once the Roman Empire to the myths, legends and rich legacy that every indigenous culture that ever existed has left us, including the sacred Isle of the Britons.

A rose by any other name, She that epitomizes the sacred feminine is still known, revered, feared, despised and honoured, depicted in every phase of womanhood from cradle to grave, from spring to winter; she whose image can be seen in every face that lives with her magic locked tight within every pore of our being.

I have thought for a long time about the concept of 'Dreaming the Goddess', what it means and what it might represent and, amongst other things, she is the quintessential and eternal life force that pulses through my veins. She is everything that I am and I am everything that she is.

As children we are shaped and conditioned by those about us who in turn are influenced by their own experiences. This creates our social norms and the environment in which we live. As children we trust and follow instinctively, we do not question how we are being influenced, we do not fear or recognise that those around us may be flawed. As we reach adolescence the Goddess is raging from within to be independent and free, to make her own mark on the world, to be loved and acknowledged. So we will, depending on our upbringing, go forth to fulfil our destiny in the world, wherever that might take us.

But what of our dreams as we mature and then grow old? How do we see ourselves? Do we just accept what we are told, conforming to the expectations of others, sacrificing a little more of ourselves each time as we feel helpless, standing by, watching the sand of time quicken its flow?

'Dreaming the Goddess' is about the true aspiration, focus, personal development and the acceptance of us as individuals and as women. We are the Goddess manifest, we are the sacred feminine; the Goddess gives voice to our hopes and fears, our dreams, aspirations and nightmares. She is us, who we are. How we honour and love the Goddess should be a true reflection of how we view, honour and love ourselves. She is the true reflection that you see when you look in the mirror, and what you see is a true reflection of yourself. You will see a representation of how you see your beliefs, how you honour, love and understand yourself.

But what do I mean when I talk of women's magic, mysteries and craft? It is every thing that represents the feminine, the knowledge we are given about our sex, our bodies, how to behave and how to live. The inner mysteries are how we feel, how we communicate, how we see the world and what we offer via our life experiences. Our gifts and essence can be translated into pure craft, is in our natural gifts, our monthly bleed, pregnancy, childbirth and menopause, our instinctual knowing with our children and loved ones and our capacity to heal others, our capacity to openly love. Of course it is not all about being fluffy bunnies - women are fierce, warriors in their own right, fighting to the death in some cases to protect those they love and causes that seem just and warranted. They are the huntresses. Isn't there a saying 'the female of the species is more deadly than the male'? Women, just as much as their male counterparts, are protectors and providers for those they feel a responsibility to, and this natural aspect of the female psyche should not be forgotten or demonised.

Our spell-craft is woven into our daily lives in the domesticity of raising our children, nest building, cooking and brewing, sewing and weaving and any other creative endeavour of our choosing. We are always planning, looking ahead as well as applying all of our talents into our professional work. In this framework we need to be aware of our personal perception and the deeds that we aim to manifest and implement as a result. I would also say, more importantly, it is also about the manner in which we engage and implement the deeds that determine our individual and collective craft.

We can often see the bigger picture (or at least we think we can) and like most females throughout the animal world we can hunt and protect and will fight when threatened or provoked; we are the ultimate warriors in certain circumstances and we should never forget how strong we are emotionally, how we can withstand the pain that comes with giving birth to life and letting those we love pass through the gates of Annwn and into the land of the dead. I believe that at those points we can find ourselves hovering between the worlds, close to both life and death and it is our inbuilt strength and personal weave that determines the outcome.

In 60 CE, on the sacred isle of Anglesey, the Roman legions crossed the Meni Straits. Their mission was to massacre the Druid priests of the Britons and destroy their last stronghold on these ancient isles. On a beach some call the 'the shores of slaughter', the warrior Druids fought and died. But the Druids who were the first line of defence and called on and met their Gods that day were the Druid priestesses, 'the Furies', as the Romans called them. They were dressed in black robes, armed with swords, spears and axes. Screaming into the four winds, they fought with valour, with magic, with undying belief, understanding what was expected of the sacred feminine. They died on that beach, staining the rocks, stones and sand with their blood so that the spirit and Gods of this land would not be forgotten, so that they as women would not be forgotten.

It is said that to this day that no Druid priest will walk upon the shores of slaughter, for it is a place of the priestesses, steeped in their magic, their ritual and their sacrifice. Of those that survived the barbarity of the Romans that dreadful day, legend has it that sanctuary was sought in a place known as 'The Blood Red Cave', a place woven with their magic, their strength, their craft and their mysteries. This is an essential thread of the web that I believe can still be woven as brightly and as strongly as ever it was by women today.

Do I know all of this to be a fact? No I do not. But do I believe in the power of what they fought for, the symbolism, myth and legend of these women? Absolutely I do. It is real and, legend or not, there are many aspects that we do know to be true. The place, the cave, the invasion and the fighting women are all true, so the rest I will leave up to you to decide.

It is this undying essence and the ultimate sacrifice that those women and all the other tribesmen and women made that that demonstrates the core of women's craft. It gives us a focus and an opportunity which can enable us to reconnect with that powerful energy in all its aspects, acknowledging that their sacrifice was not in vain so that we can shout from the rooftops "we are still here".

The rituals of women are a celebration and understanding of all the facets of the sacred feminine, manifesting them into reality, working energetically with the connections that exists between all things female and bringing them into being, giving birth to the concepts and the ideals, dancing the cycle of life, death and rebirth, alongside the sacred male energies. At those sacred times we are at one with the natural courses, the season and the earth, we are drawing on our inner knowledge and understanding and we are performing a service on behalf of the greater community, tribe and family and ourselves. I am not denying who and what I am at these times and I am not ashamed to use my natural gifts and work energetically as part of the whole infinite universe.

When we are studying the traditional Goddess archetypes we can see more clearly the connection that we were talking about earlier. Our ancestors understood the need to create a focus that represented the desired or feared aspects of the Goddess/ sacred feminine. It would seem that they had the ability to break down the differing and complex components of personality and existence, simplifying them to enable a more direct connection and clarity of focus. I think we can put the argument that this is because they saw everything as an extended facet of themselves and therefore of life itself. They understood the complexities and the need to externalise that connection and therefore to manifest it into reality. In doing so, I believe that they acknowledged the sacred masculine and feminine in all things.

In other words, if we are an extension of all things and likewise all things are an extension of us, we can identify and connect with the analogy, for example, that we are the seasons of the year: we are the Maiden Goddesses, Bride, Blodywedd or Vir and they in turn can be thought of, at specific times and identified with, as being and representing different facets of our individual personalities or of our basic human needs. If we take this concept a little further, we can then see that just as they represent the Maiden aspect of the Goddess personified that they can also represent the spring of our life as well as the season of the land. They are, perhaps, the inspiration and the childlike qualities that we sometimes forget. They are our aspirations and our dreams not yet met. They represent our creativity and our innocence as well as our vitality and health.

Our emotions and the essence of life itself are manifest within the deities of water, the seas, sacred springs and wells, babbling brooks and rivers such as Sabrina of the Severn, Danu of the River Don, Sulis of the sacred springs of Bath Spa and Brigantia of the Derbyshire and Yorkshire moors. The connection can be felt as well as seen, for these are also places of magic, gateways to the other realms, places to be revered or feared, but always places to be honoured.

We are made up of over two-thirds water; it is an essential element in who and what we are. It can be said that we came from water, the primal soup from which all things emerged. Our own personal journey of life starts with us being held tight within the sac of warm nurturing waters, our mother's womb. It is here that we stay waiting for the time until we fight our way out, longing for air to fill our tiny lungs signalling we are truly alive and we have been reborn; our first birth in this life time and yet we can still consider ourselves reborn into this world because in truth we are the sum total of all those who went before us.

We are also the moon throughout her phases, waxing, full and waning. We are the original cauldrons, our wombs the vessels of inspiration and creation from which life springs forth. In truth we are amazing and magical, astonishing in our gifts and abilities.

An idea that I thought about whilst soaking in my gorgeous Lush *Karma* bubble bath related to pro-active therapies that I had been involved in, for example, psycho drama whereby we use the grandmothers' time line. Through this process we support women to travel back to meet their great grandmothers and to hear the message that she passed down the line to the present day. This is an extremely powerful tool and can be extremely emotive and emotional for the individual as well as those supporting and contributing to the person's timeline. In most cases many of the women may have no personal knowledge of their great grandmothers and little of their actual grandmothers. The pictures that they draw and the images of the women of their ancestry is to all intents and purposes the creation by them of specific female archetypes. These will have a personal and significant message and relevance to them, enabling the women to aspire, honour, learn and make sense of their own lives. They are, in effect, manifesting the spirit and creating the representation that is most relevant and accessible to them.

The archetypes can represent anything from strength, determination, enterprise, inspiration, creativity and individuality to weaknesses, fears, desperation, failures, restrictions and abuse. As with the Goddess, the archetypes are aspects of us and the sacred feminine, and they too represent our aspirations, the things that we might need and wish to bring into our lives or dispel from our lives. So on many levels the time line provides us with an opportunity to create, communicate and interact with a personal archetype. The timeline also empowers and enables the individual to make the Goddess/archetype person-specific, providing insight and closure, bringing the whole of who we are into the present, recognising that we are the sum total of those that have gone before.

So does this support the suggestion that all aspects of the God/Goddesses are based upon our ancestors? Have we in fact based our Pagan practices and deities in what and who we think our ancestors were rather than the actual reality? In truth we cannot in all honesty know, for example, about their strength, knowledge, weaknesses or the true nature of their lives. Perhaps we are just creating and using an inbuilt survival mechanism, born out of an inherent need and made up of ancestral DNA and memory. Is it this primal memory then that enables us to connect and establish a personal and relevant relationship with who and what we are? I don't have the answers to these questions but I feel that they are important for us to ask and to explore.

The Goddess sometimes seems a nebulous concept, generic in how individuals approach her and who therefore comes across as a wishy washy idea that provides a broad spectrum of ideologies with often a confused identity attached. It has been suggested to me a few times that the male deities are worked with more specifically, particularly by men. Men find their Gods, identify with them, giving them names and embracing them wholeheartedly. Perhaps this is due to familiarity with the existing Christian God and all that male energy that is accepted and well known within our social consciousness. Women do not generally appear to do this. We do not appear to give name to the sacred feminine that we personally identify with. We may know the names of goddesses, but we do not personalise them or find our own Goddess that we work with and identify with and grow with through the seasons of our life with. Liminality as a concept of being a place or person that is otherworldly and ethereal, translucent and beyond us is a valuable perspective and not to be underestimated, but for that person or place to remain vague and veiled and on some level untouchable is not helpful nor is it conducive with singing the song of self.

It has been argued that the rise of the feminist movement coincided with the rise of the reconnection with the Goddess. From the suffragettes of the 1900s, the sexual revolution of the swinging sixties and the free spirits of the hippy trail to the warriors of the Greenham Common in the 1980s, you will find women who politicised and fought for the rights of women, digging deep in to their ancestral memories to fight injustice and redress a balance so that we could openly sing the song of the sacred female once more.

I have asked many women from differing backgrounds, during the process of writing this book, the questions "who is the Goddess for you?" What does this concept mean and how do you identify with her?' Their answers surprised me. It seems that most women, at least the women I asked, do not identify personally on the whole with the concept of the Goddess. They were able to give me the stereotypical image of who she is and what she represents, but interestingly they did not see themselves as connected with her and nor did they see themselves as representative, in any way, with the concept of the sacred feminine. For the most part 'She', (the Goddess/sacred feminine), appears to be a high ideal that is somehow out of reach.

I have included a few of the monologues from the women I spoke with and I should stress that they came from different backgrounds and spiritualities which included Druid, Christian and Hindu:

"The Goddess I suppose is up there above everybody else, she is very knowledgeable, wise, she is the leader, the big mother, the big guru. She has a big personality and is very beautiful. I don't identify myself as being anything like her, but I would like to be!"
Claudia. (Catholic, March 08).

"The Goddess represents beauty and magic, she is powerful. I don't know how I specifically relate to her, I suppose she calms me down when I am stressed, but she is separate to me."
Carol. (Christian CE, March 08).

"The Goddess is somebody to be adored, she is full of power, full of grace and humility, she is just a very powerful woman. I am not like her, but I would like her adoration, I would like to be worshipped, I'd like to be her."
Hazel. (Pagan March 08).

"The Goddess is the strongest, stronger than the male God, she is everything and the whole of the women is the Goddess. The Goddess lives inside the woman because all life comes from the woman's womb...and that's why men don't like it."
Rick's Mum. (Hindu, March 08).

"The Goddess is someone to look up to she is a warrior and is based in all things feminine. She is a very strong person, she is a leader. I don't think I can relate to her, I am not worthy, I am not strong enough."
Barbara. (Druid. March 08).

"I don't believe in the Goddess, but if I have to answer she is a mum, she is caring and guides you and is a teacher. She wraps you up and is nurturing. But I don't identify with the concept of the Goddess at all and I don't see any connection between the Goddess, the sacred feminine and myself."
Julie (Christian. March 08).

"The Goddess is in all nature and is in her connection with nature. She can be seen in the love of all other women and she is a real entity who teaches us to have self esteem and she teaches me to love myself. I don't see myself in her but I know she is in me. She is the most beautiful and highest part of me and she teaches us via craft, it is her calling card. She is not passive and she calls to all women and men if they listen."
Lisa (Pagan March 08).

"The Goddess is inspiration, power, knowledge, wisdom and self being. I am the concept of the Goddess, she brings herself into your body and there is an acknowledgement of who you are. It's about honouring, love, belonging and having faith. It's being who you should be, you are the Goddess and it takes a bit of getting used to!"
Harri (Druid March 08).

I was very grateful to these women for sharing their thoughts and for being so honest and open with me. It was interesting that many did not identify the Goddess as representing them or being them, and that somehow she was a concept out of reach and unreal. It reminded me at times of women who spend their life gazing in the glossy magazines, criticising and pulling themselves apart because they don't resemble the size 0 models and therefore do not consider themselves as beautiful and therefore a proper woman (there have been times when I have been in that category).

But how can we truly know the Goddess if she remains in shadow and not seen in all her guises or acknowledged fully when she should be? When at the times she is seen, she is reduced to a stereotypical image that is not always appropriately challenging or assertive in context with the aspect being honoured (time of year etc.) but instead is kept out of reach or nicely wrapped in a convenient little box that is beautifully decorated and that is not offensive to anyone's sensitivities. Perhaps we are not yet, as a society and as individuals, comfortable what she is and what she represents. As women we should not only dream the Goddess, but honour and live the Goddess, which means loving, honouring, understanding and not being afraid of being ourselves.

JOURNEYING INTO THE CAVE OF THE DREAMING GODDESS

Part 1: The Journey
(Play back Part 1 taken from Chapter 1, or read out the transcript to assist you as you journey).

In the Cave of the Dreaming Goddess we have time to think about how we see ourselves and be positive in focusing on how we want to be, as well as accepting how we actually are. This is a place that we can take time out to shatter our own illusions of ourselves that stop us from seeing what others see. It is in the Cave of the Dreaming Goddess that we are able to detangle ourselves, our lives and our relationships from who we think we should be from the reality of who we actually are and can be. The Cave of The Dreaming Goddess is a place to overcome restrictions and self doubt. It is the grounding place at the centre of our existence, it is the place of just being, it is our bodies and it is the land upon which we walk. Within this cave we do not worry about being afraid to be who ever we want to be and exploring who we truly are.

Part 2: Into the Caves

As you enter the Cave of the Dreaming Goddess look around, familiarise yourself with your cave. How is it decorated, if at all? What does it contain, if anything? How comfortable are you being there?

Focus on the meanings of the cave and what it has to offer you and what it is telling you about you. See an altar carved into the wall, what is on it, if anything? Know that you can create whatever is relevant to you. This is all about you whilst remembering at all times this *is* you. Who visits you when you are in your cave, if anyone? What wisdom, messages and lessons are they sharing? Remember there is no time limit with meditation other than the one you set yourself. However, when you are ready, think about what you want to take out of the cave with you. Is there anything of importance that you need to create after you leave the cave? Perhaps something you need to place within your cave on your next visit? Maybe there is something that you will need to remember so that you can bring about change in your life? Remember the cave is only for you and only you can decide what resides within it and what you bring back with you

Part 3: The Return and Awakening

Use the transcript provided in Chapter 1. Awaken from your journey happy and refreshed.

RITUAL OF SELF WORTH, EMPOWERMENT AND RECONNECTION

This is a beautiful ritual which can be a solitary practice or adapted as part of a healing or group ritual. I have used this gentle ritual for re-connection after trauma, abuse, surgery and serious illness. I have also used it as a rite of passage for the menopause. It can be as simple or as complex as you want it to be.

The Blessing

- **Water**: In a pool of water that has been blessed, stand naked. Pour the water over you gently washing it all over your body. Know that this is to wash away the pain, hurt feelings, the harm, the feelings of ill health and all other things which are affecting you. (You can use your bath if it's easier. As well as blessing the water I infuse it with appropriate herbs and flowers).

- **Air**: Step out of the water and if you are outside allow the air to embrace you fully, if not use incense as a representation of air. Turn around with your arms outstretched and smudge yourself and as you do. Trust the strength of your own mind to give you the clarity to see the situation, to free your mind of all ill thoughts. Allow the strength of your own mind to place all harmful memories where they can be positively dealt with without further harm. (Make sure to choose appropriate incense, eg. frankincense. Place charcoal into a fireproof dish and when white hot place your incense upon it. You can stand over it allowing the coils of incense to engulf you or just hold the dish and smudge yourself in whatever way is best for you.

- **Fire**: Walk between two flames (maybe two small fires or two candles) and as you do ignite and honour the inner warrior that has given you strength, courage and the will to continue. Always know and fill yourself with the love and the beauty that is the sacred feminine of you.

- **Earth**: Hold a blessed crystal of power, perhaps rose quartz, amethyst or tiger's eye; all of these represent healing, clarity and protection, strength and courage. Standing barefoot upon the earth, know that you will be nourished, protected and nurtured. You will move forward and thrive, empowered and stronger than before, so embrace yourself as you would others.

Anoint yourself with the rune symbol of *Gar* representing all elements in balance, good fortune and stability in all things. (*Gar* is a diamond with a large cross over the top ensuring that the lines of the cross extend past the lines of the diamond.) This is a traditional runic blessing and can be repeated as many times as necessary.

Chapter 8
THE CAVE OF THE CRANE BAG

Awenyddion
Wise and all seeing woman,
Her wisdom held in secret places
The crystal lights her way
And mirrors her power, her illusion, her beauty.

She of bone and feather, staff and drum
Always shining her light
Her vision is clear and focused
Her cloak of feathers spread to protect and keep us warm.

She is the secret mother, all knowing mother
The watcher and the listener
Know her by her truth as wisdoms are pulled
From deep within her sacred crane bag,
And her cauldron true.

In a dream my grandma had made me a soft suede pouch decorated with bead, bone and stone. She told me that everything I need was within whenever the need should arise, but that I should make one in my waking time.

My grandpy walked from behind her in the clearing that appeared out of the mist of the Fair Folk. He told me to look to the lesson of the kingfisher because I can learn from him and he has something to tell me. Along with the grandmother crane the kingfisher is of the three realms, the keeper and finder of the hidden mysteries seen and unseen, above and below, within and without. Call on him, he will help you whenever you need because "I am kingfisher as your grandma is crane and you are of both of us".

Grandmother Crane

She who flies with arms outstretched and holds all in her mouth, with feathers lean and strong her bounty assured, creative, healing, nurturing, giving birth and bringer of new life, she who represents fertility, reward and abundance, she who flies between the worlds, a messenger of the Goddess, a messenger of the underworld, of secrets, sexuality, the sacred feminine, of being and of knowing. She is the ancient grandmother and sacred guardian of the midwife's fire and the blacksmith's forge, holder of the secret words and the knowledge of truth. She understands the alchemy of self and manifestation as she flies from on high into the otherworld, betwixt and between she plies her trade and sings the soul into being and into the long sleep.

I will tell you the story of ritual and intent and you kind folk will make your own minds up, but hopefully take something away with you that resonates and has opened your mind to the fire within your head, to the possibilities of what is, what was and what could be again, that your eyes will open to the secrets that already reside within you, perhaps dormant but regardless at the same time continue to pulse through your veins as necessary as the air that you breathe and the water you drink.

As you find your way to your internal cave, listen to the sound and the embrace of the Crane Grandmother and hear the shattering hammering of her constant companion, he of the fire and the anvil and recognise his song of creation, his song of deep magic and the song of self.

"I am the blacksmith of legend. I work and hold the magic of the blue flames of this land, hammering the changes into being. It is I who will forge the gateway to the next place of your lives and to the new season that must always follow the old."

In the oak grove within Swithland Woods I had this experience in the July 2007. Within my mind's eye and in a place of liminality a woman holding two spears walked from between the trees. She, I understood, was the warrior spirit of the land, of the sacred feminine and of me and all women. She stood before me with spears firmly thrust into the ground in front of me providing a gateway which I know I was to walk through at some point.

Within the Cave of the Crane Bag and the place of high mysteries, share a day and a night of ritual and questing. Allow a natural release, be strong in your banishment of what cannot serve you any longer and embrace the acknowledgement and renewal that this freedom will bring. This is always a place of personal initiation, of testing yourself in the shadow of who you are and in the perception of who you think you are, rather than who you could be, should be and perhaps who you really are.

"To walk between the spears is a commitment to the truth and that which is necessary to enter your life with confidence and self-belief. This is your time to learn to shapeshift with wisdom and understanding, to utilise the alchemy within and of the deep and old mysteries of magic held within the land, seen and unseen."

I knew that walking between the spears would be a pivotal point in my life, the wisdom of knowing that it was time to stop hiding and to embrace the spiral path that is my life. In doing so I would then start to pull together the experiences and knowledge gained. This was my time to step out of the shadow whilst understanding the importance of its existence.

As I walked between the spears, I walked into the cave. The crane bag was in front of me in the centre, it was open and waiting for me to look inside and all the time it was telling me to not fear it. I accepted, understood and embraced the uncertainty of necessary change. I realised that the crane bag of my high mysteries had always existed with the heritage of my blood, with the lessons taught by those who raised me, with the eternal contribution of all that had been before me and, most importantly, by my own making.

The warrior spirit no longer stood before me. Instead the swirl of the night air and the remaining wisps of heat from the day's sun wrapped around me ensuring I understood that I was held now and always, and so began new chapter in my life.

It is often said that in the classical days of the Druids of Britain, they carried upon their persons at all times bags of power made from the skin of the magical and sacred crane. Their bags would be full of the magical and necessary tools of their trade.

To the Druids the crane was (and still is) a sacred bird representing the connection between sky, earth and water, the three realms, which included mind, body and spirit as well as the land of the ancestors and the land of the living. The crane was the bringer of new souls and the guide to the underworld of the dead. It was known as a bird of the midwives and blacksmiths, of the birthing fires and the secret places.

Within the crane bag the Druid placed his tools of divination, medicine and healing, teaching and ritual. It was the bag of personal power which could be used to secure whatever the need might be at any given time. However, the Druid needed to be knowledgeable and wise in the practice of his trade and so his bag was a symbol of wisdom learned, gained, shared and experienced and its magic was recognised and revered.

Many times I have run workshops where by participants have made their own physical crane bag as an important talisman of their personal power, representing the magic and wisdom of who they are.

As a child I did not have a crane bag as such but I did have various little boxes and bags filled with my precious things, stones, herbs, lace and so forth. My grandma often made my little boxes and would fill them full of things that she knew I loved and which represented part of me. On one such occasion she filled one with handmade lace bobbins, beautiful butterfly pins and silk threads, stunning and magical.

However, sometimes in life, situations, circumstances and issues arise leaving us feeling out of our depth and perhaps ill-equipped and inadequate. At these difficult and challenging times we often need to look for the answers, the resolve and the courage from within to do whatever needs to be done. So into our metaphoric crane bags we delve. What experiences can we draw on when we find the courage to place our hands within the bags? What natural abilities can we pull out and utilise? What hidden resolve and inner strength can we draw out of the bags this time? And what tools of our trade, of our very being will we find?

How many times have you felt powerless and left not knowing what to do for the best, when suddenly you pull off a mini miracle? That is the magic of the crane bag. It will always provide what is required at any given time. It is that inbuilt and natural intuition to sense and know, it is the natural instinct to know what is best, what needs to be done and the wisdom to know when to act and when not to act.

The crane bag represents the secret place where we sometimes hide, talents and skills out of the sight of others, which can include even ourselves occasionally! It is within the crane bag that we store all of our secret knowledge gained since the beginning of our time but also acknowledging and building on the wisdom and knowledge of those who went before. In short it is one of the truest magical essence and spirit of what makes us, us.

You cannot help but to have this place, a place where you cannot lie and cannot pretend because there is nobody to fool, nobody apart from yourself listening, so despite what you might say and do in the outside world, the truth will always be the truth, will always be heard and will not be silenced, for the crane bag holds all, light and dark, good and bad, the secrets of all that is you.

The crane bag represents connection and the knowledge of that connection. That is the true magic. I was told by my grandpy the "magic is knowledge that I have but you do not, or it is knowledge I have given you but you have not understood". I have always kept that in mind and used it as an important mantra when working, teaching or performing ritual.

True magic, as with life, is alchemic in all forms. You can take completely unconnected and different ingredients, like when baking a cake, bring them together, mix them, cook them and then before you eyes they will change into something completely different, united and as one form. Sometimes heat is needed to bring about the chemical fizz that is required, sometimes cold, like water into ice. The reaction to and blending of differing elements is the alchemic process at work and one that we can see in creation of all things. The truth of the alchemy is we are it and it is us. Nothing is static, none of us are the same as the day we are born, we continue to change and adapt and become different in our abilities, knowledge and experience until the day we die and what happens then is another book. This is alchemy and that process begins at the point of conception, taking differing aspects, blending them and creating something new. That is life, that is survival, that is creation, life, death and rebirth.

The Cave of the Crane Bag is the place within us of high mysteries. It is the place of all that is hidden and all that is seen, for they are not necessary the same thing. It is also the place of sexuality, desires, intuition and magical practice. The cave is the place that enables you to learn who you truly are, as well as to not be afraid of your shadow but instead to work with it.

The secret of the Cave of the Crane bag is that we can view it in the same way as we would the roots of the tree which give us nourishment and strength. The crane bag is a place of secrets and of our own hidden world and is both of the light and of the dark, just as roots can be. Within its bindings, the Crane bag holds the sacred essence of knowledge of who and what we are, as well as who and what we know we should be.

Within my crane bag I place things that have meaning to me and are of personal empowerment. I hold the things that aid me, feed my spirit and hold my diverse abilities until they are required and within the crane bag they can not get lost if I don't remember them until I have need.

I view the cave as a temple as well as a liminal diary that records my life and a library of knowledge that I can access if I apply myself and I can be bothered to take the time.

For all of us the truth and wisdom of the caves will always be personal. The point of the Cave of the Crane Bag is that it holds the tools of whatever is required and relevant at any one time. We can often forget that we already have the answers and forget to look within the cave with our internal crane bag.

The high mysteries of life require the natural alchemist to emerge from within and brew the elixir that will sustain us through our lives, personal, professional or social.

Natural insight, intuition, learned wisdom and knowledge gained by experience are all part of the recipe that allows us to shapeshift and become whatever is required of us. We truly walk between worlds, be that motherhood, partnerships, sister, friend, lover or work colleague. You are the magician that needs to gain in confidence, understanding that you have all the pieces of your puzzle. It is up to you to manifest your life into being, singing at all times the song of self. The lesson of the Cave of the Crane Bag is the magical practice of learning about and knowing self.

It is sometimes hard to explain the concept of how magic works and the impact and implications that can manifest as a result. Within the craft we talk of intent and the manifestation of our will to shape our own or another's reality. This is the purest form of alchemy and carries a massive amount of responsibility with it. Examples of this include the blessings we bestow, the creating and invocation of sacred ritual and the healing we give and or receive, but how many of us truly understand the process? Is this a case of belief? Can we say that to believe in something only means that we only hope, that we have doubt and therefore do not actually know? Perhaps we can suggest that a lot of the energy that is given out or received is often ignored and thus does not reach its mark or if it does, is not sustainable. Of course this also means that the energies worked with, where the intent is not clear, can go awry, so we must always remember cause and effect.

The ancients seem to have understood the truth of mystery and the liminality within which it is sometimes held with great insight and wisdom. In viewing and holding many of the aspects of the sacred mysteries in a way that can be described as betwixt and between, the ancestors ensured wisdom was kept safe and alive, whilst ensuring that they remained available for those who truly have eyes to see and ears to hear. We might not always like what we see, hear or learn but this means it is all the more important as a place where we must not be afraid to look. I truly believe that we, from time to time, must learn to embrace both the light and the darkness that resides in all things because one cannot exist without the other and therefore neither the light nor the darkness should be perceived as being more important than the other.

In my world, craft/Druidry is a living tradition, an experiential tradition, an oral tradition. Its roots are deep and forever fed by the richness of time shown in our myths, legends and in the ages-old traditions and customs that have been passed downs over the millennia. Over the eons craft/Druidry has been known and recognised by many names, but it is as old as life itself and we are as old as it.

I understand this as being an essential part of who we are, of our psyches, our need and ability to adapt and change. The craft is about sharpening and honing our senses so that we may use those natural tools in order to survive. It could be argued that we have lost some of these core abilities in today's world, but for me practicing, learning, teaching and even writing this book is about continually re-establishing those connections. The core of any magic, and by definition our magical craft, is about sitting down and thinking about how we actually connect with the world around us. As a magical practitioner the craft is about understanding how we resonate on the same energy levels as those around us, be it human, animal, vegetable or mineral, and the magic then is about recognising and enabling us so that we can draw on those energies bringing them within and sending them without.

Druidry and the craft are for me about the natural alchemy of energy exchange that can be perceived as one of the purest form of magic. We ourselves, from the point of conception, are made up of specific components which when brought together cause a chemical reaction transforming the original components into a different entity, which of course is us. But after we are born the process of change, development and ultimately shapeshifting continues until we are no more and then the cycle begins again.

Nothing is static, energetically all things merge and transcend their original form so within craft/Druidry we are able to establish those portals and take those first tentative steps through the doorway that the portal has provided so that we can experience and see all of creation and the world around us in a different light. The magic is in understanding that we are all connected and it is only an extension of ourselves that we are looking at, communicating with or working with. That does not mean that there is loss of individuality or that we lose our own song: it's quite the reverse. Instead you are merging your energy, giving you a deeper and more varied insight enabling you metaphorically (and perhaps actually) to sing in harmony.

The uniqueness of the alchemy, this truest of magics, is that nothing and no one is the same. We are all individuals; all one offs, unique in our creation and form and as a consequence we all will sing our own song. It is remarkable that even though the same ingredients may be placed into the cauldron of creation and the process of creation remains unchanged but what is birthed at the end of the process is still unique and individual. Yet if we sing our songs together the harmony that would be heard would be breathtaking and staggering in its completeness and beauty. Everything would be in balance. This is not impossible because all we would be doing is what comes naturally, so how hard can that be? Very, it would seem, for a lot of the world, at this moment in time. After all isn't balance one of the main focal points and aspirations of Druidry/craft, and is that balance not symbolised naturally to some degree within the equinoxes?

In following our truth we admit to our aspirations. I believe that in some way our aspirations can be interpreted as reflections of our higher selves and so can be achievable and realistic goals to set ourselves.

The beauty of the craft and of magic is that it is not static, it is not fixed; the ebb and flow is maintained quite clearly within its ever-changing parameters. It has been my experience that in studying your craft and in implementing the ethos of the infinite universe, you will not be able to help yourself, you will have to move, to shift and flow, to change and grow along with the nature of all things.

As an individual I have been so blessed over the years with the enlightened people that have come and gone from my life. These people, who have all been so different, have inspired me, loved me and supported me and sadly some have ended up disliking and challenging me. I once had somebody who I considered to be a dear and beloved friend who said something that I thought was quite profound at the time. He was responding to my distress at moving forward in my life in a positive and pro-active way. It was at an intensely difficult and painful time, when I had lost my faith and direction. He said *"The best place to start is with what you don't know"*. What good advice, especially when following a demanding and often perplexing spiritual path. For many years I did not fully embrace all that I am, all that I have been, nor did I appreciate my potential - all that I could be.

If things we believe are not challenged and questioned we run the risk of becoming fixed and complacent. If I am being truthful here, I became the latter. I never questioned my Druidry, my belief system, my path, because the truth of it is, I never felt the need - or should I say wanted to. However, I can in all honesty say that I have now been to that place. My faith has been tested and way beyond endurance at times. As a result there was so much that I came to realise that I really did not know, especially about myself. In living and walking my truth

I understand that my craft/Druidry is who I am. I do not cease to be because I am asleep; it is only a different facet of my being. Nonetheless I would describe myself as having been a shadow of who and what I really am. I can't put it into words really it was just a feeling that I had always managed to hide part of myself, never fully embracing the whole of who I was, always afraid of others' disapproval, that perhaps I wasn't quite up to the task or just plain good enough. None of the above is reality really; they are just my fears and personal control dramas. Even so, walking and talking ones own truth does comes to mind, if you know what I mean. For a long time I had found my truth but I didn't really know it. There has been so much in my life that has given me joy and great happiness but it was the personal crises and the chaos that proved to be the impetus that switched on the light. The different aspects of me, my life and resulting experiences each provided me with their own gifts, both from the dark and the light times, providing me with a pivotal period of growth.

JOURNEY INTO THE CAVE OF THE CRANE BAG

Part 1: The Journey
(Play back Part 1 taken from Chapter 1, or read out the transcript to assist you as you journey).

The journey into the Cave of the Crane Bag is one of experiencing the magic and wisdom of self. It is the cave of the high mysteries of the hidden and the seen. It is about your sexuality and your gender, the alchemy of intuition, knowledge, ritual, learning and experience. In this cave you learn to work with both your dark and light aspects and how not to be afraid of your shadow, balancing all aspects within and without. The Cave of the Crane Bag is the roots of the tree that holds you strong, sinking deep into the warmth and nurturing earth, providing nourishment and strength to sustain you on your life's journey whilst singing the song of self.

Part 2: Into the Cave:
Once you are comfortable and your breathing is relaxed enter your cave in the same fashion as before. Ensure that you are clear which cave you are entering.

As you enter your cave look around and find the crane bag. What does it look like? What is around it? Is it open or closed? Again make the cave yours, is it comfortable? Is it warm? What are your impressions and senses within the cave?

Pick up your crane bag, spend time with it, what can you see? Is there anything you need? Is there an insight that might be gained? Look inside your bag and see what your can find. You might be surprised what is there.

Ask your questions or add what needs to be added, bring back what needs to come with you.

Part 3: The Return and Awakening
Use the transcript provided in Chapter 1.

SEWING THE BAG OF ABUNDANCE
The crane bag is the wise one's essential bit of magical and personal tat. It is that which represents their wisdom and ability. All that is ever needed resides within it. It was never allowed to fall empty and ensured the connection with the three realms remained at all times. When you open and place your hand inside the crane bag you are, to all intents and purposes, entering the underworld because the crane bag represents the underworld which holds all of the hidden secrets of the higher mysteries to which we wish to access.

By its very nature it is a talisman and a charm, practical and personally relevant to the individual, it is an identification and validation of you and all that you are. It is an item of ritual through and through and is made by individual initiatory and ritual practice.

It can be argued that the crane bag represents what is needed, what is sacred and the wealth and abundance of life. That is how we can use it in our day to day existence as well as magical practice. We all have personal items, symbols and experiences that have brought happiness, strength, good health and perhaps wealth. Within your bag you would gather suitable items that represent the things that are important to you, that perhaps you want to encourage, develop or protect. They don't have to be big and they don't need to mean anything to anyone else because this is your bag and represents you and your three realms of mind, body and spirit.

To make your own personal crane bag is easy and relatively quick. Once you have chosen your fabric (suede, leather or wool, it doesn't matter because it is what means something to you), cut an oblong shape, fold in half and then sew up the sides. If you hem the top all the way around but leaving the ends un-sewn you should be able to thread cord through to make a draw string bag.

Decorate your bag with symbols, patterns, beads, shells and feathers, again ensure it is relevant to you, make it as simple or as intricate as suits. You might prefer to leave the bag just as it is without additional embellishment and that's ok as well.

Once you are satisfied with your bag place within it the items you have chosen confirming the intent behind each item and what it represent for you. Once you have finished it place it somewhere appropriate, or maybe keep it with you at all times. When the need arises look within your bag and pull out what you need, be it intuitively or proactively.

When I have made crane bags in the past I have ritualised the process. I always start at the dark of the moon, sewing my bag and weaving in my spells of intent as I go. I then leave it upon my altar until the new moon, (approximately two weeks). Then from the new moon until the full moon I decorate my bag again, reinforcing my spells of intent as I work. I also gather all of the items to be placed within the bag and charge (energise) them upon my altar. On the night of the full moon I dedicate my crane bag and then place my chosen items within, ready for whenever I need them.

Chapter 9
THE CAVE OF THE PRIMAL CALL

Hawke
Who knows my name, I scarce know myself
For I am the Hawke of a bygone age
Those who thought me gone may think again
As I speak from the depths of my crystal cave

Dead I am not, but in eternal rest
In my beautiful tomb that I made for myself
Except for the help of my raven love
I placed myself here through my blindness of lust

I who danced with dragons both red and white
And walked with the Bear from the dragon's lair
I who cleared the way for the Bear to come
To join with the land, to make it one

But listen carefully all you children of Earth
To an old timeless man once known as the Hawke
The mists will come and the dragons will fall
And I, with the Bear will walk once more…

There is a wood I know, not far away, a wood held deep in shadow and feared by all those who dare to venture in, an ancient place of ritual and sacred practice that guards its secrets well, except to those who understand the twist and turns of its paths. We are few in number now, and as the new order rises form the ashes of the old, I suspect we will retreat further into the shadows, and deeper into the last remnants of a world many claim to have died thousands of years ago.

Within the cave that was carved out millennia ago by the Ice Gods I stand, hidden and secret in my practice. I gaze into my fire and wrap my fur cloak about me, for I feel the chill of winter fast approaching. My Gods are fading fast, and their descendants are now coming of age and will soon be strong enough to stand in their own right. Whilst I understand this is the way of things and I know that my Gods are in truth just giving themselves new form, new identities so that they can still move around in the world that is instead of the world that has long been laid to rest in the mist of time, I am struggling to do the same.

The alchemy of magic and the true nature of the hidden mysteries is a natural and instinctual way of being. Some of us have differing skills within the wheel that turns us and we may apply our craft in different ways but we are nonetheless magical creatures driven by the ebb and flow that dictates our path. We are the walkers between the worlds, the dream weavers and healers, we are the Gwyddon of yester-year, named and re-named over the thousands of years since the day of our creation. We are the bridge that allows others to cross and we are those that remind the world of what has been and will surely be again.

My words are just whispers on the breeze, a faint heartbeat that vibrates around you, not meaning to intrude and yet hoping, all the same, that you hear it and it gives you comfort. We are still here...

The light is fading outside now and I know that soon the night hunters will begin their work. Am I one such creature? I have often asked myself this question and perhaps in part I am, but in truth I know it does not come naturally to me, that is not my way, but maybe I need to learn. Perhaps the time has come if I am to thrive and survive in this world that I see swirling and growing before me.

***

It is the early hours of the morning, I am tired and anxious and waiting. I was asked to help the dearest of old men, my grandfather, to let go and midwife his soul to the four winds, the Summer Isle and the place of our ancestors.

When he knew his lung cancer was terminal and his health slipping from him at a terrible speed, he asked me to help him. He felt that he would fight long past the time when it was right for him to do so. He wanted the rites of his spirit to be sung into the next world and he said I was the only one in the family he could ask to do this. It was an honour, it was a burden that weighed me down, lest I disappoint and let him down, but that I also gladly accepted.

I spent most of my time with him as his time drew near. He spent most of it in and out of consciousness or talking with relatives, loved ones and friends waiting to take him with them, so it was a great surprise when he suddenly came to and looked at me and requested that I go to the temple at the bottom of his bed, that 'they' would not allow him to go any further until they had spoken to me.

He was irritated and almost distressed when I said I couldn't see where I was meant to be going.

"Just go to the bottom of my bed, they are in the centre of a stone circle by an altar…just go please"

I did as he requested and as I reached the bottom of his bed I hit what I can only describe as a wall of ice-air. It was cold and yet welcoming. It was so very strange. I could feel it penetrating my very being as it in engulfed me, letting me know that it was going right through me. I stood there for some time, not quite knowing what I was to do. I can't say I saw or heard anything but there was a definite connection and a sense of knowing and belonging. Perhaps that was all I was meant to experience.

"I still can't hear or see them Grandpy, but I can feel them and I can sense them" I called out. He smiled at me,

"That's alright, that's alright, and you can come back and sit by me now. They will let me go now". It nearly broke my heart as I saw the tears rolling down his checks.

"Yes Gramps it's alright to go, just close your eyes and let all those waiting for you greet you".

I lit the charcoal in readiness and readied the passing-over incense that had been made by a friend for this very purpose. It was all happening so quickly now and I couldn't believe that this most beloved of men was about to pass out of my life in this world.

A few more difficult breaths and I held his hand and softly sang his soul to leave,

"Let it go, travel well my love, let the four winds take you there. Leave this body, let your spirit go, no more pain, let your spirit flow". There might have been other words I sang but to be honest it was whatever came in to my head and was relevant at the time.

As he slipped away I smudged his body with the charcoal and incense and chanted the following:

In the east the silver stream,
May your spirit know its inspiration and dreams fulfilled.
Blessed be.

In the south the fire gleams,
May your spirit know its warmth, love and joy.
Blessed Be.

In the west the bough bends down,
May your spirit know its healing and flow.
Blessed Be.

For in the north all the quarters crown,
May your spirit know its way home to the Summerlands and
the place of your ancestors.
Blessed Be.

The Primal Call

What is the 'primal call'? It can feel like another one of those banded about phrases that can appear innocuous, difficult to define and to express adequately and yet at the same time, feels like an eternal ache, a connection so deep, its roots are perhaps lost to us in the mists of time.

But the primal call can be seen as an organic and living tradition. It can be an unexplained feeling or emotion of connectedness, of belong and of knowing, that flows and gushes up from deep inside of us. It has a long established history that grows richer with each and every generation. It is like a tree with healthy roots that are in bedded deep within our sacred landscape, with a trunk that is strong and rises high above the earth and withstands the test of time, with its branches reaching out and able to bear the weight of all of the luscious foliage and any animals that may dwell there. For we are the tree and therefore we are, like the tree, the sum total of all that has gone before us. We harbour and protect the seeds of the future, so to deny them is only denying ourselves and who we truly are.

Perhaps the primal call is the collective consciousness, the ancestral DNA screaming thorough our veins. Perhaps it is the natural instincts that can be found in all things that are or should be a constant in our lives, reminding us and binding us to what is most important. Then again perhaps it a little of all of the above, manifesting at different times dependent upon our needs, openness and recognition.

The primal call is the call of nature in its purest sense. It is the call that you can feel in the pit of your stomach when danger is felt or deep emotion surfaces. It is the ability to connect on the necessary levels to enable survival. It is the connection to those that have gone before and it is the undying connection to the land and the Great Goddess that shelters and provides for us regardless of our abuse of her.

The primal call is raw in all its facets. It does not allow us to forget who and what we are and it will manifest at any given time without warning and can be one of the truest reflections of our state of being. It can be in the call of a couple's lovemaking, the painful call of grief contorting a body in physical pain or the comforting sense of belonging we can feel. It can be the recognition of places, people, the inexplicable knowing that we sometimes have and the pull that that takes us on an unexpected journey. This is our truest connection when we are acting out of instinct rather than conditioning.

The primal call within divinity is no different. It is affected and dictated by the same considerations and as such is just as much a necessary part of who we are as anything else in our lives. In defining the primal call we are giving structure and focus and a means of understanding and coping. But the question still stands; why do we have this connection and where does it come from? More importantly, how does it fit into our understanding of contemporary magical and spiritual practice? For this we need to find what we can think of as an original source which we can perceive as one of the primary threads that have been spun over the millennia. For me, one such thread can be seen in the Ceridwen's or even the Universal Cauldron.

I have learned that it is from the shadow (and ultimately the darkness) that all things -including clarity - are developed and birthed. It is from the blackness of Ceridwen's cauldron that all things that are hidden take shape and are made manifest. The shadow that sometimes can give us such fear is not always what it seems and instead is only the doorway that leads us to the darkness and the all-knowing blackness. This is where the universe, in all her magnificence, holds all beginnings and all endings. This is because Ceridwen as one of the names given to the Universal cauldron is one of the true manifestations of the primal Goddess. It is this primal Goddess and her universal womb that we should understand as the true cauldron of creation and destruction. This Cauldron is the place from where all that we understand as being within our sphere of comprehension, to have emerged. It is from here that all of our understanding has always been centred because, on an unconscious level, we know that our ancestors and all those who have ever believed that we have come from the stars weren't wrong. The primal instinct, the primal Goddess if you like, is the bedrock that forms my foundation; I am the representation and current incarnation of all that went before me right back to the original and primal creation of all things.

I can never be anything other than what I am. Within in this alchemic mix I incorporate all my destructiveness but my recipe also includes all of my beauty and all of my creativeness, my inspiration and my aspirations. I will always need reassurance, love and support but to appreciate these things is a two way street. I will always be in need of feeling and being safe with the freedom to explore and express myself including the right to disagree and express my sadness, disappointment and anger.

The primal call is the blood in my veins that makes me who I am. It is the fates, it is my identity. It is my ancestry. It is my pain and my pleasure. It is my happiness and sadness. It is my love and my knowledge, my creativity and inspiration. It is me. It is you.

Over the years my grandma took me to many sacred landmarks, to Stonehenge, Avebury and various springs and wells amongst other places. She told me that Stonehenge was a place of the ancestors and of winter solstice, a place to ask for the light to return and a place of honouring as well as one of the gateways to the underworld. She said that the stones were guardians and represented once living people who were honoured by their tribes and who acted as go-betweens between this world and the Gods of the underworld. As a child I totally got it.

Henge is a living temple built by our ancestors and therefore deserves to be treated as such. On one of our visits to Stonehenge we made a little offering and buried a ring. My grandma said I would always be joined to this place and it would once more be joined to me. I have always liked that idea and it has somehow always felt right.

When I started my periods at a very young age, she talked to me of the magic within, of giving my blood back to the land. Grandma told me that women used to collect their moon-blood to use as fertiliser in the garden which helped the plants grow stronger and bigger. She made me a box of special things to help when I felt wretched and my tummy hurt, little things like a beautiful hairbrush, chocolate, bath salts, lace and ribbons. The most important gift she gave me though was to tell me that my moon-blood was not an illness but that it was a natural part of the cycle and that my body was naturally expressing the ebb and flow of its own tide. I often think how sad it is that young girls today are still taught that this beautiful gift is a curse and dirty.

I cannot put into words how eccentric, mad, naughty, rude and sadly spiteful my grandma was. If you have ever heard the poem "When I am old I shall wear purple and a hat that doesn't match," she was all of that and much, much more. She would often be seen in pink florescent tights and matching leotard and little black dolly pumps running up and down the stairs in her block of flats. She once called the fire brigade out to rescue her (she wasn't worried about my grandpy I might add), because she and only she was snowed in. What she failed to mention as the fire engines could be heard screaming down the road, was that she lived on the sixteenth floor of said block of flats! One last example I can give you, which was the *piece de résistance*, happened during a memorable Christmas shopping trip in an extremely busy department store in Clifton, Bristol, which I accompanied her and my great aunts on. If I can just set the scene, the store was in the height of the Christmas shopping frenzy was heaving with people. All around stood the most lavish and elaborate of displays made up of beautiful baubles and expensive decorative items. Grandma, obviously bored with shopping, decided to pretend to faint and did so right into the display tables, knocking everything and everyone flying. Of course attendants came running from every direction. She was very dramatic and deserved an Oscar and asked for her smelling salts to be wafted under her nose. It was chaotic and surreal and straight out of a Noel Coward play. She was helped to her feet and a chair was fetched along with a glass of boiled water with a slice of lemon that she had demanded.

There was a huge audience by this time and I and my aunts

were in fits of laughter, partly out of embarrassment but mostly because grandma had everyone where she wanted them and people were waiting on her hand, foot and finger. When we finally left the store, leaving behind a scene of mass devastation in our wake, grandma turned to me and said,

"Poor people, Michelle, are mad. We are middle class and we are therefore eccentric, and being eccentric means you can get away with so much more and have so much more fun". She winked at me, laughed and walked down the road as fit as a fiddle and unbelievably pleased with herself.

For my sixteenth birthday, grandma had arranged 'a surprise', as she put it. You can understand why I was more than slightly worried at this prospect. At any rate she had hired out the whole of the sauna at a top fitness and beauty club so that she could talk to me about becoming a woman. I have to be honest I was mortified at the time. My grandma was not a shrinking violet as you might of guessed and the thought of seeing her naked in a public arena - and more to the point her expecting me to get naked - was horrifying, let alone thinking about what she was about to say to me. But she was not a woman to argue with, it was too much trouble,

"Don't be ridiculous Michelle, there is nothing wrong with your body and nothing I haven't seen already and haven't got myself," is all she would say. So there I sat in my first sauna, having this rite of passage with my grandmother, naked!

Once she had poured a fair amount of water on the coals (and what seemed like twenty tons of Olbas oil) I could barely breathe. My eyes stung and were streaming and my nose felt like it was on fire.

She talked to me about her life, the sadness and her regrets, of the babies she lost through stillbirth and miscarriage. So tragic and sad, hearing how one time when in her twenties she had gone into labour but the weather was terrible, snow storms and drifts had made it impossible for her to get out or for anyone to get in. My grandpy tried to walk in the blizzard to find some help, but whilst he was gone, grandma gave birth to a stillborn child. So tiny, she said, so transparent that she could see through it. She sat holding her baby in the palm of her hand, on her own, with nobody to help her for the longest time.

She told me of her dreams and of the work she did during the war. She talked about my mother and how proud she was and how disappointed she had been when mum gave up her dreams because she became pregnant with me but she told me I was always loved from the moment I was born, that I was beautiful and that I should never be afraid of who I am. She told me that I came from a line of extremely strong women who knew their own minds and that there was nothing in this world that I couldn't do if I believed enough in myself and was prepared to work for it.

I cannot do justice to the way that she was, how funny she was and how wonderful a storyteller she was. In fact both of my grandparents were. I can only tell you what she said. Looking back it was the most amazing gift, but I don't think I truly appreciated it at the time, in fact I know that I did not.

I do not believe that either of my grandparents thought of themselves as either Druid or witch - that would not have been something they would ever have associated with. Their generation still lived in an age were such words had frightening meaning. Craft was hidden in many ways or relabelled to fit in with accepted norms. Perhaps they would fit into our understanding of how we see cunning folk but it doesn't really matter, they just were what they were and knew what they knew.

My mother on the other hand openly taught us hedgerow craft and our house was always alive with music, arts and crafts, brewing and making. At midwinter my mum always took us out greenery gathering and we would make our own garlands to decorate the house in time for Yule. Our house always looked different to other people's houses at this time of year. We did not have the multi-coloured tinsel or foil decorations as was fashionable, instead our houses smelled of the fresh pine and apples that we had scooped the middle out of and sprinkled with cinnamon and then stuck a candle into so that when it was lit the heat from the candle created the most gorgeous smell of warm apple and cinnamon that permeated throughout the house. There were also the orange and clove pomanders and pomegranates. Beautiful greenery decorations of holly, mistletoe and ivy were everywhere, pinecones and spectacular table decorations with the scent of frankincense and myrrh, and lest we forget, the mulled wine and cider along with home baked mince pies. I can see, taste and smell it all now. It was a grotto of magic and wonderment and from an early age we understood the significance of the greenery being brought into the house and the importance of what it represented.

Every solstice we always had an open house when there was a meal or buffet and all were welcome. Everybody who came always marvelled at the decorations and commented at how amazing it all was. This was my mother's pride and joy and a ritual that she always went over the top with and still continues to do so to this day, as I do now in my home.

My grandfather said "We are the guardians of the knowledge (magic) to ensure the survival of the people". Quite grand words for such an unassuming man but believe me when I say there was true integrity and a deep understanding of service and sacrifice, of walking between the worlds and the responsibility that this has come to represent. It a constant reminder of who I am and why I walk this path.

Ancestors

In the dark of the Mather's womb,[2]
Moss covered, earthen chambers,
The light of the Ancestors
Will shine for you

In the light of the Ather's gaze,
All around the circles of stone,
The voices of the Ancestors
Will speak to you

Hear them call
Feel them near
Know that they are in you

In the cover of the Druid's grove,
Sacred rites by sun or moon,
The presences of the Ancestors
Will guide and support you

And in the silence, when you're on your own,
Full of fear not knowing which way to turn
The spirit of the Ancestors
Will always inspire you

Hear them call,
Feel them near,
Know that they are in you.

---

2   Mather means Mother and Ather means Father. The Order of Pendragon claimed to have been used the terms in their rituals. I wrote this poem after reading about them.

JOURNEYING INTO THE CAVE OF THE PRIMAL CALL

Part 1: The Journey

(Play back Part 1 taken from Chapter 1, or read out the transcript to assist you as you journey.)

This is the meditation to enter the Cave of the Primal Call. When you enter think about who you really are and who do you think you should be. What knowledge do you hold within the fabric of your very being and can you access the vast library of the ancient ancestors? What is your DNA memory and can you find it within yourself? The primal call is what shapes you, your looks, your features, your talents; it is the call of the grandmothers and their stories. It is an unbroken line to the beginning of all time, connection and freedom. It is the Samhain of the year and of our lives. It is the natural and instinctual side of who you are.

Part 2: Into the Caves

As you enter the cave know that your ancestors were here before you. Look around you and see the paintings and the decorations on the walls, the symbols, the messages that are perhaps left for you to find. What artefacts have they left? What gifts are there to inspire and empower you? Find the hearth at the centre of the cave and sit for a while. Think about why you are there. Think about those that have sat in your place before you. Acknowledge their wisdom and hear their songs and stories echoing around you. Understand and feel their strength and courage. Know that you now join them and share their gifts but have not yet finished your own weave and so will come and go as you need to.

Part 3: The Return and Awakening

Use the transcript provided in Chapter 1. Awaken from your journey happy and refreshed.

CRONING RITUAL

Several years ago I was privileged to preside during the croning of a dear friend. The croning is the rite of passage taking us from the mother phase of life into the time, wisdom and the eternal beauty of the grandmother. This is celebrated within tribe, family or community and for us she was being croned as a member of the Anglesey Druid Order as well as also reflecting where she felt she had moved to within the hour glass of her own life.

It was a beautiful Samhain (Halloween) night, cold and crisp with a stunningly clear and starry night sky as a canopy above our heads. We were on the Island of Anglesey and our ritual was held between the tides on the beach not far from where we were staying, in a cave representing the sacred feminine and the universal Mother Goddess.

The following is the blueprint of her ritual and can be replicated or adapted to suit your own needs.

To the Cave

- The men of the order prepare the cave.
- The cave is lit with candles and the cauldron full of sea water is placed within the centre of the temple space created. A bowl with blood/wine, a pot with blue pigment, bowls with offerings of milk, acorns and water as well as a fire dish are all positioned within the temple space.
- The women arrive at an agreed time to process across the beach to the cave.
- The woman to be croned walks between the women and is veiled. The women carry torches to light the way.
- Some of the women drum the heartbeat of the land as all chant and call to the ancient grandmothers so that the spirit of place and the ancestors can hear the call to empower the rite.
- As we approach the cave, the men have lined both sides of the

processional way into the cave. Their backs are turned, they cannot see the initiate; she cannot be known to them.

- The women all enter into the cave. The men remain outside and guard the entrance.

Ritual within the Cave:

- The women stand in a circle around the initiate and a circle of intent is called, including elemental aspects, ancestors and spirit of place. Then the call is again made to the grandmothers of ice and Gogorwen, the serpent mother of Mon and Britain.
- The initiate is asked if she is ready to take the step into cronehood.
- A circle of acorns is made around her, representing the potential she had as a child and the wisdom she has gained thus far.
- A circle of mother's milk is next placed around her, representing the nurturing mother that she has been but understanding that now is the time to nurture herself.
- Lastly a circle of sea water is placed about her, representing the nourishment of being and the ebb and flow of all things.
- The veil is lifted from the initiate's face and she is challenged "Ancestor of the future, what does this step mean to you and what will you do with your gained place in the coming years? What is your stated intent in your croning?"
- The circle of women are asked if they are satisfied with her answer and if 'yes' the rite continues.
- The presiding woman faces the initiate and makes the following statement: "You are no longer fertile; your time of bleeding so others might live is over. You have sacrificed enough, others will now sacrifice on your behalf"
- The offering of the blood/wine is poured into the cauldron of sea water with the blessing of the mothers.
- The initiate is then marked on the forehead using the blue

pigment, the sign of the crescent moon, "You are now Bone Woman" and she is presented with a bone.

- The initiate is marked next to the crescent by the mark of the full moon, "You are now Stone Woman" And she is handed a stone.
- Lastly the initiate is marked next to the full moon with the sign of the waning moon, "Eventually you will be Back to Earth Woman" and she is presented with a small pouch of earth.
- The woman presiding stands in front of the initiate and states the following: "You have stepped through the doorway and have accepted your place amongst the elders. Leave this place knowing that the wisdom of the Crone is that you are whole and complete as you always have been. Know that you are still maiden, mother and grandmother. Nine of our Sisterhood I acknowledge you, know that you are honoured here".
- One by one all of the women acknowledge and honour the crone.
- All elementals, ancestors and spirits of place are thanked and the circle is closed but its intent not broken.
- The crone leaves the cave and is welcomed by the men who also acknowledge her and honour her by presenting her with a yew staff. They then carry the cauldron of blood and sea water down to the ocean's edge and the ebb and flow is allowed to seal our spell of welcome and intent of initiation regarding the croning of a very special and magical woman.

Chapter 10
THE CAVE OF THE HEALING POOLS

Earth, divine goddess, Mother Nature, who dost generate all things
and bringest forth ever anew the sun which thou hast given to all
nations; Guardian of sky and sea and of all Gods and powers;
through thy influence all nature is hushed and sinks to sleep...Again,
when it pleases thee, thou sendest forth the glad daylight and
nurturist life with thine eternal surety; and when the spirit of man
passes, to thee it returns. Thou indeed thou art rightly named Great
Mother of the Gods; Victory is in thy divine name. Thou art the
source of the strength of peoples and gods; without thee nothing
can be born or made perfect; thou art mighty, Queen of the Gods.
Goddess I adore thee as divine, I invoke thy name, vouchsafe to
grant that which I ask of thee, so shall I return to thy godhead with
the faith that is thy due...Now also I make intercession to you, all
ye powers and herbs and your majesty; I beseech you, whom Earth
the eternal parent hath borne and given as a medicine to health of
all peoples and hath put majesty upon, be now of the most benefit to
humankind. This I pray and beseech you: be present here with your
virtues, for she who created you hath herself undertaken that I may
call you with the good will of him on whom the art of medicine was
bestowed; therefore grant for health's sake good medicine by grave of
the powers aforesaid
Prayer found in Latin in a twelfth century English herbal (British
Museum MS Harley 1585) and quoted in *The White Goddess*,
Robert Graves, Faber, London, 1961

Deep healing waters, never-ending serpent rising from within the Mother's womb, gently, gently it washes over, breathing and sighing the ebb and flow of life, taking you, forever moving, on your eternal life's journey.

Immerse yourself completely within her arms as she rocks you back and forth, See the elixir of primal energy crash in waves upon your soul and know the truth of the Serpent Mother, she of rivers, springs, brooks and wild seas, the eternal blood within your veins, source of all that has been, all that is and all that is still to come.

Step into her embrace and she will surround you, hold you, bathe you and heal you. Step into her world and she will take you deeper and deeper until you both are one.

My Experience

I had been ill and was awaiting news from the hospital as to whether or not I needed treatment. I had been to the cave a few times where the older woman had given me some healing. She was able to reach inside me and then place a poultice of herbs that she had prepared over the infected area. She told me that the herbs would draw out the impurities and help to remove the disease. She then placed a sort of lantern within the darkness that was once occupied by my womb. This amazing wise woman told me that I should focus on this light, allowing the flame to grow within, spreading throughout the darkness, dispelling any harmful entities whilst energising me throughout my body. I was instructed to return daily for the poultice to be renewed and this I did for several days and it was on one of these visits that I experienced the following:

I always journeyed to the cave in the same way and my guide was always waiting, however, he now left me at the standing stones outside the cave and never ventured in. The older woman, more often than not, would be sitting by the fire in the first cave, waiting, and then after greeting me would lead the way down into the inner sanctum.

This particular day we made our way across the river and

straight to the fire. This day the fire was not on the raised stone platform but on the ground. I was handed a cup made from some kind of horn and told to drink as I needed it and should make this for myself in my world. The woman told me that it was a honey drink with juniper, mistletoe and rosemary. The juniper was to cleanse and warm my blood, the mistletoe to re-ignite the life and energy within my body and the rosemary was to purify and give protection.

It was then that I felt able to ask her name.

"Anumunda," she answered, "now come and lie here." She pointed to what can only be described as a stone altar and I did as I was told. (For those who know me please don't be so shocked - it can and does happen occasionally.)

Anumunda then looked at the light that she had placed within me a few days earlier.

"It's not very bright is it?" She looked at me sternly. "You must work on illuminating the fire within you, let it energise you because the brighter the light the more energy will be provided". I duly apologised and said that I would try harder.

Anumunda then turned her attention to the old poultice that she had placed there on my last visit. As she pulled it out I couldn't believe how dark it was and it looked like a lump of slimy ooze; it dripped onto the floor as she placed it into a wooden bowl. I remember feeling quite shocked and horrified by the sight of it. She said nothing at this point, just smiled at me and continued with her work. At length Anumunda explained that she would also be packing the top of my vagina with sphagnum moss so that none of the ooze could drip down and infect me further and so stop the disease from spreading. She then replaced the old poultice with a new one.

Helping me down from the altar, she led me back to the fire.

"You need to learn how to draw energy from the fire," she told me. "You can boost the flame within and keep yourself nourished, especially through the dark months and you must do this regularly. Now," she continued, taking hold of me and ensuring I was facing the fire in the right way, "Hold your hands out and face your palms towards the flame". This I did. "See the energy exchange and push your energy to meet the fire. Right, now let the fire in and let it feed you, always remember it is a very important part of you."

The feeling was quite amazing, warm and bright, and I could feel it flood through all of my body. I could also feel the flame within shine and flare up, adding to the feeling of being re-energised. Don't ask me why but it was at that point that the bone talisman came to mind.

"Can you tell me what the bone talisman that you gave me is for?" I asked. Anumunda laughed at this question and responded by saying that there were some things that I needed to find out for myself but she took the talisman that I was now holding between her finger and thumb, holding it at the top on the flat round bit and then stuck it into the flames of the fire. I have to say I did not understand her meaning at all and she obviously knew this because she burst out laughing again. As quickly as her face lit up with laughter it was now suddenly very serious.

"Get into the fire", she said. I began to object when she said again, "Get into the fire girl, there is no need to feel afraid". But I *was* afraid, in fact I was extremely scared and worst of all I could see that she wasn't going to take no for an answer. Slowly I edged toward the flames. I could feel the heat and it was already burning my legs, but I had decided to trust my intuition and that had told me to get in to the fire as I had been instructed.

As I stepped fully into the fire everything changed. The fire flew up around me, covering the whole of my body and flared up over the top of my head. It was fantastic, amazing, I just don't know the words to fully explain the experience and how I was feeling at the moment. The flames were ferocious and yet they did not hurt me in the slightest. Around my body the flame was almost brilliant blue with orange flames on the outside of that.

"Doesn't it make you feel good?" shrieked Anumunda. "Don't

you feel alive? Remember that you are alive, feel it, let it become part of you. You are alive!"

I remember turning around in the flame; it truly was a remarkable feeing and I felt elated and somehow free. As the flames continued to engulf me I heard a soft and almost lyrical voice on the wind, in the flame, above and below and in me. The language I did not know, but it felt like a charm, words of significance, spinning a web all around me. I remember calling out,

"Who am I?"

"Don't you know?" came back the reply, "Remember who you are".

Suddenly, as quickly as the flames had engulfed me they were gone and I was standing once again in front of Anumunda. With all of my clothes gone, I stood naked before this other worldly woman.

"Will you teach me?" I asked, a rather stupid question considering the circumstances.

"Isn't that what I have been doing?" She smiled as she answered.

"I feel like I know this place, like I belong," I said. Again Anumunda smiled,

"Well that's perhaps because you never really left." It was a surprising answer and one that I didn't really know what to say to.

At what point I had forgotten my nakedness I am not sure, but I had, and again I had a sense of freedom with that feeling. Anumunda signalled to the two younger women who I now noticed had been standing quietly to one side, watching what had been going on. They both took an arm either side of me and guided me away from the fire and the lit torches to a part of the cave I had not seen before.

Water fell from the rocks above our heads into a beautiful pool that in this light looked as black as coal and yet it had a shimmer that looked slightly eerie. I was taken to the edge of the pool where I noticed steps leading down into the blackness of the water. Anumunda signalled again, but at me this time.

"In you go." I did not attempt to argue this time but as I stepped into the water the shock of the ice cold hit my body like a thundering train. I hesitated and began to step back out of the pool.

"No!" boomed Anumunda's voice. "Go right in and fully immerse yourself, there can be no half measures." Her voice was stern. So slowly, and I mean very slowly, I lowered myself into the dark waters of the pool. I cannot put into words adequately enough the pain of the cold, the gasping for air because my lungs could not work nor the complete numbness that shot through my body.

"Doesn't it make you feel alive?" Anumunda called. "Feel it and become one with it. Let it in and flow through you, let it feed and heal you. Remember who you are. Remember you are alive. Do you feel alive?"

I don't think I quite managed to answer. My body responded in the water allowing me to lift my feet from the floor and make a feeble attempt to swim. I ducked my head under and again the shock of cold knocked me to such an extent that as I surfaced gasping for air, desperately trying to breathe normally and failing, I was convinced that I might pass out.

Finally I was instructed to step out of the pool. The two younger women helped me up the last few steps. My legs were like jelly as I stood on the side of the pool dripping, shaking uncontrollably, completely numb and with my teeth chattering. I was absolutely freezing and desperately trying to understand why I allowing myself to be put through all of this, but somewhere from deep inside I knew it was important and significant.

Anumunda smiled at me and then nodded to the other women who once again took my arms and guided me to my next challenge. This time I was taken to a little door in the side of the cave wall. The door was opened and I was pushed forward into a small hole of a room and I noticed that my pouch was on the floor.

I turned back towards the door and the only warmth and light was shining out from behind Anumunda. Her hand was outstretched and open and the bone talisman lay in her palm.

"You may need this." I took it from her, slightly bemused, and the door was closed leaving me practically in darkness.

The floor was earth and felt damp under my feet. My body was whipped by the winds that raged through a round window cut into the back wall. I could hardly move, my was body numb with cold, freezing and still shaking. The wind cut right through me with my wet hair stinging my back and face,

"Doesn't it make you feel alive?" the wind screamed. "Who are you? Remember your name"

"I don't know who I am. I am so cold!" I yelled back into the darkness, now huddled on the floor, shaking uncontrollably.

Under my leg I could feel twigs and leaves and so I felt around. I could feel the wind was blowing more fiercely now, savagely cutting into me and continuously screaming at me in the darkness. My only thought was that I needed warmth and that I must have fire.

Scrabbling around on my hands and knees I quickly gathered as many of the twigs and leaves as I could find. It was then that I remembered the bone talisman that I was still clutching tightly in my hand. I knew what to do. I blindly felt around for my pouch. I found it and fumbled to get the flint out of it. Then holding the flint in the same way that Anumunda had shown me, and close to the little pile of twigs and leaves, I struck the flint over and over again down the ridges of the bone talisman. Tiny sparks flew out and finally caught. My fingers were bleeding from flint, but I did not care. The flames raged higher and higher. The heat seared through me and then it happened, I remembered.

"I am Michelle, I am me!" Tears fell from my eyes "I am Me!" I called out. The door swung open and Anumunda stood before me smiling radiantly.

"Welcome Michelle."

Gently she helped me from the floor and out of the room where the other women were waiting. Between them they bathed me in warm water that smelled of woody herbs. After drying me they anointed my body and painted beautiful patterns and symbols upon my arms, torso and face. They wrapped me in a material of soft fleece and hung my pouch from the belt they then tied around my waist. As they finished, one of the younger women, hugged me tightly and whispered into my ear,

"Welcome home Michelle."

"It is time for you to go now," It was Anumunda who spoke now, "You have passed your initiation; there is nothing more to do this day." I remember smiling to myself - initiation, how mad is that? It all made so much sense and I truly felt humbled and yet proud.

"Why do I feel like I belong here?" I asked again.

"Perhaps because you never truly left," was my answer.

No more was said to me and I left the cave in my usual fashion, but with a sense of knowing, and as I made my way back my thoughts were already fixed on my next visit and what other mysteries I might learn.

A Very Witchy Affair

I spoke with my sister Frances to recall our childhood. I wanted to ensure that I wasn't looking through rose tinted specs and that, for the most part, my memories were accurate. I was so surprised by not only her memories of me and what I got up to, but also of things I had totally forgotten about. It was wonderful.

Frances often sat for hours in Mum's vegetable patch at the bottom of the garden, playing with the Fairy Folk. She also had her most special of friends given to her by the Fair Folk to look after and play with her and they were her little green dogs. I can say no more about them, except to say that she gets upset if people claim they were not real and describes then as looking a little like greyhounds. One of my most endearing memories is always seeing her with an extremely muddy face, particularly around the mouth, sitting amongst the runner beans and carrots.

In the 1970s I spent long summer afternoons with my friend Julie and her granny and my little sister Frances, in their garden. Julie's parents were the high Priest and priestess of a coven in Keynsham (North Somerset) and they were good friends with my mother. Frances and I are pretty sure (we both seem to have separate memories) of Mum being part of their coven, but for some reason unknown to us she now denies this. Any rate, we would always follow Julie's granny around picking flowers that we always had to smell and taste (probably herbs, looking back). She always sang to the plants as she picked, spitting onto each plant in thanks for its sacrifice, giving back of herself with gratitude for the gifts the little plants offered, she would tell us and as she did so we also danced and sang. Then we would all sit on the steps at the back of their house, place our gatherings into a very large bowl when Julie's granny pounded them and mixed them all together. Granny chanted over the bowl as she worked and again we danced as she did, it was such a happy time, I can still see her sat on the steps and it always makes me smile. I just wish I could remember her words.

I loved being there. I loved listening to her and I always smelled of nature and aromatic herbs when I returned home. One particular day I remember coming home and in the kitchen were Julie's parents and a very tall man, dressed all in black, with dark hair and a beard. I did not like the look of him and there was something about him that scared both me and my sister. If I am completely honest, Julie's parents had always scared me slightly in any case - they always seemed so very tall, slim and stern. They would get very cross if Julie and I went anywhere near the very old and slightly crooked oak chest that sat under the window in their front room. There was one occasion when I plucked up the courage and I did have a peak inside and I didn't see much except for a black velvet cloth that covered whatever was hiding underneath, but on top was a beautiful shining sword that appeared to glisten and radiate light whenever the sun caught it through the window. I so wanted to play with it, but Julie was having kittens at this point and so I carefully and quietly pulled the lid shut. What magical things lay beneath that cloth I could only imagine but I knew they were there: I could smell them.

I can't say what was discussed in our kitchen that day, but whatever it was it was not pleasant and my mother appeared very unhappy and struggling to contain her anger. Our three guests left very suddenly and Mum turned to us and told us that we were to stay away from them, that we were not to go, under any circumstances, to Julie's house again, that it wasn't safe and that the tall man was not a very nice man. It might be a bit of an exaggeration to say Mum was scared, and even as children we were not oblivious to the seriousness of the situation.

Needless to say I didn't listen. Julie was my friend and I wanted to play with her, so a couple of days later I skipped up the road for a visit. I couldn't believe it when I got there, the house was empty, completely empty. They had moved lock, stock and barrel more or less over night. Nobody knew where they had gone or exactly when they went, but I never saw Julie or any member of her family again. My mother never spoke of them again and over the years has denied knowledge of ever having known them, but both Frances and I remember.

Empowerment and Healing

In writing this book I have found it interesting that one of my main roles over the past twenty years or so has been in working with and supporting marginalised and vulnerable people within the community, particularly girls and women. I have learned a lot about the way society, and individuals within society, operate and as a consequence the psychology of cause and effect. Just as importantly I have learned a lot about myself within this process.

Women have often sought me out to help them when they have suffered great traumas, from rape, domestic and sexual abuse to serious and terminal health issues. The work and the rituals I have been involved with have focused on individuals or groups being empowered to bring about necessary life changes. Together we are able to achieve this by supporting them to feel that they do have control in their lives, that they can take responsibility and be pro-active in their own problem solving. In taking these steps we can then start to explore possible choices that might be available and perhaps had not been obvious initially. Of course, every person's situation and issues are specific to them. Therefore, when working with others it is imperative that even though we may use the same techniques of practice, everything must be tailored to address the individual need, and ensure that we are person centred. As practitioners, we are there to provide and create a safe environment so that we can engender ways in which they, the individual, can look at their issue with a different perspective and, most importantly, take any necessary action as deemed by them to ensure their own well fare. If this process can begin we can claim that this is what it means to be empowered. By facilitating the healing of deep wounds and seeping scars we can begin to take back the control in our lives and are able to begin to look at our world differently and we are, therefore being empowered to release the harmful energies that have had a hold on us and have perhaps been stopping us from moving forward positively. However, it is worth mentioning again that at all times we should remember that the relevance of any magical work, ritual or not, that involves others needs to always be focused on the individual. In this way we ensure that our work is appropriate, accessible and person or group specific and centred.

I keep saying this, but I know it to be a truth - everything is about energy and energy exchange. Part of my role in these cases is to be the 'electrician' that helps to re-establish the flow of clean energy while never forgetting that the ownership and responsibility for that energy is with the individual themselves.

We are such magnificent creatures with a capacity to achieve astounding feats of bravery, intellect, creativity and endurance and I know that especially applies to health and self healing.

Antibiotic Tincture

This isn't something that all of you will necessarily want to try, but it is something I have always made and have given to my children over the years. It can be used as a treatment or a preventative but either way it is gentle and supports your body's own immune system. This is not to be used when a doctor's treatment is needed. Use your common sense and take personal responsibility. If you are in any doubt due to other medical conditions or pregnancy please seek advice or don't use it at all, other than enjoying the process of gathering and making your own treatment.

1 tbsp of dried Echinacea
1 tbsp of St John's wort
A handful of rose hips (prick the fruit to ensure all the goodness can be released)
1 tbsp of yarrow
I tbsp of hops
2 tbsp of honey dissolved in small amount of warm water
500 ml of brandy
Place all the ingredients into the brandy and mix. Pour into dark coloured bottle and seal. Shake every day for a month, then leave to stand for a further two months, when you can strain and re-bottle. Take 3-4 drops three times a day, either direct onto the tongue or diluted in a glass of water.

JOURNEYING INTO THE CAVE OF THE HEALING POOL

Part 1: The Journey
(Play back Part 1 taken from Chapter 1, or read out the transcript to assist you as you journey.)

The Cave of Healing Pools is just that, a place of healing, revitalizing you, a sanctuary to retreat to to recharge and nurture yourself. Have you been looking after yourself or are you always preoccupied with the needs of others? Ask yourself what it is that *you* need and allow yourself the time to actually take the required time out.

Perhaps you will find healing pools of water within your cave ready and waiting to invite you in. Allow yourself to fully immerse within them. Feel their healing powers washing away the stresses, strains and tiredness of the day. Use this place as a focal point to go to if you are combating illness in your life; this is such a powerful place so fill your cave with everything that uplifts and sings to you and your spirit, rejuvenating you as it does.

Part 2: Into the Caves
As you find your way into the Cave of Healing Pools, notice the sound of crystal water cascading into your pools. Perhaps it is time to bathe within the pool, to refresh and cleanse and to heal. Look around you and see if there anything you might want to add to the water? What is there to warm you? What is there to nurture and care for you?

This is a place to face yourself and acknowledge any necessary changes that you might need to make to your life. It is a place to retreat to and lick your wounds, to gather yourself, making the necessary space in order that you can move on. Importantly it is a place to put things into perspective and realise where they belong, enabling you to be proactive in your own healing and your own personal development.

Part 3: The Return and Awakening
Use the transcript provided in Chapter 1. Awaken from your journey happy and refreshed).

RITUAL FOR HEALING AND CLEARANCE
This ritual is one that I wrote with healing specifically in mind but is one that can be adapted for quite a few things, particularly cleansings, purifications and letting go of unwanted stuff. It is a long ritual that is performed over the course of a full lunar month and therefore needs continued focus and clear intent during this time.

This is an excellent example of sympathetic magic because it is proactive and is visual in its application and effect on both the individual performing the rite and on the recipient. Although it is not necessary that the person is present, it is important that they understand the process and the method so that they can participate by focusing their intent as well.

On the new moon make a clay figure of the individual, incorporating any relevant herbs, oils and objects. For example when I performed this ritual for a friend who was diagnosed with a potentially life threatening condition and who was facing serious and invasive surgery, I added mistletoe, walnuts and cloves, all of which have cancer fighting properties. During this process the weaving chant that I use is one that was sung by the women of Greenham Common and is still sung today by the women of Tipi Valley in Wales. It is chanted when things need to be put right, disputes stopped and hurts mended, and it can be sung as you work. I have found it to be very useful. However if you prefer to create your own chant which you feel is more relevant to your personal needs, that's fine as well:

Weave and mend, weave and mend,
Gather the fragments, weave and mend the sacred circle, sisters,
Weave and mend, O weave and mend,
Sacred circle, weave and mend.

When you have finished, place the figure on your altar or another significant site and leave it there until the dark or waning moon. Chant your intent every day over and into the figure.

On the dark of the moon place the figure into a bowl of blessed spring or river water, again chanting every day over it to dispel the illness. Leave in the water until the next new moon. The clay figure should dissolve into the water breaking down the problem, illness or hurt.

On the new moon take the clay and water mixture and offer

it back to the earth. Light a candle that has been appropriately carved with the required symbolism and anointed, and burn cleansing and purifying incenses. When they have burned down, collect the remains of ashes and wax and bury them in the place that you have poured the clay and water solution into, chanting as you work:

"Into the earth my spell is sown, this is my will, so may it grow."

You can end the proceedings here if that is appropriate, but I also adapted the above ritual for another friend who used it for somebody who was sexually violated. Elemental blessings were incorporated as part of the ritual as the individual was present and wanted to participate.

Earth: The person is standing barefoot on the earth and they are given a small pouch of earth to hold or wear. The person performing the rite states the following:

"This earth is your foundation, your security. May you nurture, nourish, protect and thrive. Embrace yourself as you would others."

Air: The person is then smudged as the following is spoken over and around them:

"May you have the strength of mind to find the clarity to see the situation, to free your mind of all ill thoughts toward yourself and any harmful memories."

Fire: Two candles or two small fires should be lit and the individual should stand between the flames as the following is called out to them:

"I ignite and honour the inner warrior that has given you strength and courage. May you have the will to continue, to fill yourself with the love and the beauty that is in truth the sacred feminine that is you."

Water: Take a bowl of blessed water and allow the water to flow over the person or if possible stand in a spring or shallow river (if safe) as the following is spoken:

"As the blessed water flows over you and through you, so may you feel the healing and cleansing of all pain and hurt. May the ebb and flow take that which no longer serves you and bring that which is needed to take you forward. Know that the tide has turned and you are truly blessed within the living waters."

Once the elemental blessing is complete the woman is anointed with the runic symbol *Gar*, which represents all elements in balance.

I like this ritual because it is so versatile and it can be adapted in so many ways, making it as complicated or as simple as is felt appropriate. I have also used the ritual for the menopause. I have incorporated the making of clay goddesses to represent the individual and the internal Goddess within and without.

Chapter 11
THE CAVE OF CAULDRONS

"It is the Spiral Dance of rebirth that brings us back to the source of our existence in the Goddess and the God...Since all life is joined in the dual deity and to each other, life cannot be destroyed, only changed or moved into and out of the Cauldron of Life".
(Ann Maura, 'Green Witchcraft, Folk Magic, Fairy Lore & Herb craft' 1996)

"You can be whatever you want to be, manifest your own reality."
(My mother, grandmother and several other important women throughout my life)

The Goddess, incubator of infinite possibilities, primal mother, the cauldron from which all is created, universal Mother of transformation and potential, she of the sacred Serpent Goddess and Ceridwen the Black Sow of Winter, the devourer of all that's seen and unseen, initiator of the uninitiated, inspirational, creative, the sacred womb of life giving and life taking.

When we imagine the true divinity, be it male or female, have we truly understood the concept that our ancient ancestors, arguably, took not only for granted, but recognised as enabling them to surpass the limits and confinements of our own existence?

The cauldron is all, the source of all power, the Awen that comes from the sacred brew of the cauldron is, the spark of life and the stillness of death. It is the beginning and the end. It is the universe of all things. It is our spirit, our aura, our strength and protection and our weakness.

Annwn is the name of the cauldron that holds the unknown and the darkness. It is the universe in all her glory and expectation, devastation, annihilation. It is the stillness of contemplation, anxiety and the insecurities before conception and rebirth commences. It represents all of the promise, including the essential ingredients to manifest all things into being. She who is the universal Mother is the ultimate cauldron (womb), incubating the necessary building blocks and components that can be brewed and exploded in the cosmic alchemy required to create, be created and exist out of all of the infinite and available potential.

The magic (knowledge) held within the mighty cauldron is the *Awen*, that spirit and the spark of life and that aspect of us that inspires, resonates and embraces all that life has to give. The ancient goddess Ur was known as the universal grandmother from whom all life descends, she who understands the fragility of our existence and demands our dedication, resilience and persistence in reaching and fulfilling our potential which can have no limits other than those that we impose. The cycle of life, death and rebirth is the gift and the wisdom of the cauldron and in return we are eternally empowered to be whatever we want to be.

All through our lives our instinctive need is to survive. This is not a process devoid of our input and ownership. We must accept personal responsibility along with recognising opportunities and potentials when they arise. We will face difficult and challenging situations that will test us to the limit. How many times have you said "I cant take any more?" or "I don't know what to do any more?" It is in those times that we often, without realizing, travel inward, looking for answers and ways out of situations and a place to retreat. Such times often result in denial, anger and the rejection of many things and people that I have held dear, but I have always had my craft, my personal magic and the natural alchemy by which I pull myself up off the ground, dust myself off and find the new out of the ashes of whatever lies at my feet. I - and many of you - continue to do it over and over again, because that is life, and life is not static.

The language by which we understand and implement magic and the practice of craft is so difficult to define and can be so complex in meaning, use and context. Much depends upon personal interpretation which in turn is based upon personal experience, knowledge and agenda. The language of magical practice and craft in general is for me in its exquisite splendour, colourful, diverse, multi-faceted and as varied in description, analysis and practice as any other aspect of the human and or universal condition. How we express our understanding of the magical mysteries can be mirrored in how we express our understanding and how we actually apply ourselves to the task of living.

Energetically and practically we are always trying to understand our own being within the cycle of existence. The consequences of personal responsibility and the universal laws of cause and effect propel us forward on the continuous path of personal development. This is a path which can only be viewed as a life long endeavour full of peaks and troughs, mistakes and achievements. If I accept that I am, along with all other aspects of our living world and the extended universe, a magical creation, then the language of magic and of craft is absolutely about connection, communication and ultimately about existence itself. To define such a vast and limitless concept is beyond the realms of my abilities. All I can do is try to understand and continue to explore my own part in the wheel that forever turns. In doing so, hopefully, I am able to gleam the necessary insights that connect me to others, to the world, universe, cosmos and to myself.

I think the ancients understood the truth behind our need for mystery, our need to quest, to be warriors in seeking, to be brave in our endeavours but I think they also ensured that the learning, knowledge and perhaps the power were reserved for a privileged few. Maybe the reasoning behind it was that everyone had their role within the tribe and those deemed to be the priests and magical workers had theirs. Perhaps the knowledge and magic of the tribe was their insurance of survival, age old knowledge, passed down each generation by word of mouth, each adding their wisdom. In this way they continued the tradition of sharing intimate knowledge and understanding of the land, hunting and healing, all locality and tribe specific, knowing that each generation would interpret and adapt the information left for them so that it always had meaning and relevance. We can not ignore that perhaps such importance was placed upon such wisdom that they wanted to protect it and they did not want it falling into the hands of hostile tribes. All of this should be considered as my own musings; we will never know for sure, but human nature has not really changed that much from the time of our ancient ancestors. As societies grew, well, maybe that is when corruption of such positions emerged. We will never know. The truth of holding any such mystery, wrapping it within a veil of protection, perhaps creating the illusion that it doesn't even exist, would suggest this would have been for good reasons, for example, ensuring its secrets were kept safe and yet available for those who had eyes to see and ears to hear. This analogy is still relevant and transferable for us. To seek the inner mysteries, to step into the unknown and into liminality, with all its perceived uncertainties, is a place where we must not be afraid to look, just as we must embrace both the light and dark in all things, because one cannot truly exist without the other.

The cauldron evokes deep and intense imagery, often emotive and stereotypical but it represents more than just the vision of a witch's brewing vessel or the medieval iconotropic conception portrayed as the chalice or Holy Grail. They are all valid, but they don't cover the complexities and depth of meaning.

I see the cauldron as the absolute primal womb from which all existence emanates. There are actually three cauldrons of being, or three cauldrons of existence which are found within land, sea and sky.

These are the cauldrons of the three realms of the great primal Mother, she who holds all, giver of life and death, eternal and never-ending, holding us on our sacred journey of life, death and rebirth.

There can be no doubt in my mind that these realms were of paramount importance to our ancestors. Alexander the Great and his friend Ptolemy reported the oath given by the Celts in sealing a treaty as thus:

"If we observe not this engagement, may the Sky fall on us and crush us. May the Earth gape and swallow us up and may the sea burst out and overwhelm us". (As cited in T.W.Rolleston's Celtic Myths and Legends 1994)

T.W. Rolleston suggested that there is much evidence to support that this oath survived in various forms down the ages.

So what are these cauldrons to us? What do they represent and what wisdom can we gain? With each of the cauldrons holding sway over us, our creation, our lives and our very existence, all separate and yet intrinsically linked, the answer will be personal and experiential but I will share my own interpretation.

Cauldron of Land: the Living Mother

The Spirit of Bone is the Cauldron of Land. On the wings of a bird we follow the contours of our sacred land. On foot we walk her wild pathways, from mountains high and caverns deep, giving us that sense of belonging, that knowing of who we are and where we belong.

The Cauldron of Land is all around us, in the earth beneath our feet, in the fauna and flora that share our space upon this living planet which that holds and nourishes us as we all come together upon an ever-changing but eternal and sacred landscape.

This is a landscape forged with breathtaking alchemy. A war of elemental forces of great magnitude clashing in unimaginable ways as they found their peace and gave quarter to one another, where time had no meaning and millennia passed in the blink of an eye, all the way back to the beginning of all things. The curves and crevasses of mountain, hill and valley, lush and fertile, harsh and unforgiving, nestling us within its very being on the living Mother's back and within her arms, protected, challenged, nurtured and inspired to be all that we can be as we sing and dance our way along the spiral path.

The Cauldron of Land, our living Mother, represents the practicalities of living and of our place upon the planet, our interaction with each other and all other living things. In the realm of land our connection is profound and deep rooted. It is from deep within her womb that we call to our ancestors, those who walked this path before us, so that we may understand and know our place within the cycle of all things, that we may understand and know our connection to all things and so that we remember who we are and where we have come from.

Upon this beautiful earth we strive and we thrive as we make our life journeys. Within the Cauldron we manifest our own reality, energetically exchanging, sharing and connecting to the beating pulse within the heart of the living Mother. This is our hearth and our home, our prosperity and our present, it is our absolute connection to the here and now, it is the physical aspect of who we are, it is our kith and kin, our tribe and our community. It is our connection to all that is sacred when giving birth and form, in whatever capacity, of holding and growing and understanding.

Within the Cauldron of the living Mother we are given the Spirit of Bone, the bones of land to provide structure and strong foundations on which we are able to build our lives. We are strong, we are adaptable and we are unique, all of which defines us as we merge within the temple of life and death and we walk, sing and dance to the eternal rhythm along the ceremonial path ways of the Cauldron of Land.

Cauldron of Sea: the Mother of Living Waters

The Spirit of Blood is the Cauldron of Sea, sacred water, raging seas, rivers, lakes, streams and springs, the primal cauldron of protection within which we will see and feel the ebb and flow of life. It is a place of magic and high mysteries, of crashing waves and shattered mirrors that can destroy, distort and disconnect our focus, as well as lift us up, freeing, healing and connecting us with clear direction and intent as we steer our way through uncharted waters. Know it as a place of deep emotion, fathoms below us out of sight, holding us as we are guided upon the tides of our very being. Know it as a place of sacrifice and defiance where there is no right, no wrong, it is just strong and mysterious yet gentle and dependable when approached with caution, reverence and knowing.

From the flow of all that is held most dear, the sacred living waters of the Mother run through our veins, necessary and vital to the existence of all life, healing and rejuvenating, washing us clean upon the shores of existence as the waves of her eternal blessings entwine us in her all embracing arms. It is here that we submerge ourselves into the depths of her flowing energy as we allow ourselves to sink into the realms of the unknown, deeper and deeper into the place of hidden mysteries and sacred knowledge. Here we are in a place of mirages and dreams, in a realm betwixt and between, held within the primal sac of creation that is the womb of the Mother of Living Waters. Here, we are safe and we are protected, given space to grow whilst swaddled and floating in a cocoon of natal fluid, waiting for the right time for us to once again emerge.

Feel the rise and fall of her changeable nature as it feeds and quenches our thirst. Recognise her mood in all guises. She can swallow all things whole or bring forth treasures from her depths. See her as a raging storm with no mercy or quarter given, or as the gentle kiss of her waves upon the shingle bringing relief and pleasure in her release and cooling. We should understand that she surrounds us, runs through us, is eternal. She can be never still and is forever moving and ever-changing.

These are the sacred waters, gateway and portal to Annwn, providing blessings and balance, truth and honour. The Lady of the Living Waters lifts her sword on high for all to see, the weapon of the cleansing waters blessed by the mother of battle and slaughter, life and death. She is the Great Serpent Mother who weaves her way through all of us and all that we hold dear as she guides our journey from the world of living into the underworld of the dead.

Cauldron of Sea, Spirit of Blood, feel the waters thick and thin that flow through the bones of who we are, connecting all that we can be, whilst ensuring that within this most sacred of cauldrons, we survive within the embrace of the Mother of Living Waters.

Within the Cauldron of the Mother of Living Waters we are given the Spirit of Blood, blood that signifies our connection to the ebb and flow of the living waters and our transient nature where nothing is static as all things need to move and change, be adaptable and fluid in their outlook. The Cauldron of Sea is our personal mystery, our understanding and our knowledge. It is an experiential knowing, often indefinable in nature, and yet it is part of who we are. We are creatures that can walk between worlds: this primal cauldron is our journey as we seek, understand and do.

Cauldron of Sky: the Universal Mother

The Spirit of Breath is the Cauldron of Sky and the universal Mother that hangs above us, an awe inspiring canopy of dreams, aspirations and longing. This is a cauldron of wondrous sights, a continuously changing canvas that can paint our moods, our imagination and our intent.

It is the universal womb of brightest day and darkest night as Brother Sun and Sister Moon shine down bestowing their blessings upon us. The sun will provide us with warmth, comfort and growth, whilst the moon, in her turn, will provide insight and vision through the darkness of sleep, growth and wishes that empower and channel clear thought.

We close our eyes and see her stretch before us. Blackness descends as we float away amongst the breath-taking celestial wonders that light our way. This is the cauldron of intellect and inspiration, infinite and limitless, amazing in its construction as the Universal Mother encourages us to reach for the stars and dance with the giants of possibility that make up her nebulous brew.

There are no limits within the endless possibilities of the universal womb. It is from her holding and motherly containment that the Spirit of Breath and Universal Cauldron enchants our skies to energise and feed us. She ignites the Spirit of Blood and the living waters that connects and flows through the Spirit of Bone that creates and shapes all things and thus life in its many guises is born, lives and returns to her arms upon death.

Gods of thunder, rain and lightning clash on high to replenish and bless what lies below, not always peacefully, their rage loose, their fury unleashed, unrepentant and sometimes unforgiving. But rainbows can arch and fill the skies, ribbons of colours merging and blending, symbols of hope and peace, sacred gateways of magical promises of hidden treasures to be sought and found.

There are shooting stars and comets tails, flaming rocks that fall to earth, highlighting our fragility, our wonderment and our sacred questing as we allow ourselves to look into the cauldron. Are we not eternal seekers, pioneers of the unknown, watching the skies day and night for new frontiers and new horizons, enriching us in the infinite spiral that enthuses the raging fire within our heads.

Within the Spirit of Breath Cauldron, the universal Mother, we are given all elements combined, all the potential of creation. We are held from on high as the spark of life is ignited within all of us. We can have no end or beginning because we are all connected and all birthed from the primal source. We are the wind and the breeze in our ideas, thoughts and aspirations; we are, with each breath we take, the manifestation of our own realities. We are the indefinable, the dreams, the alchemy, and the illusion. We are governed and affected by all things within the natural and perceived unnatural world; we are affected by the sun and moon, the stars and the planets in the night sky. We are absolutely universal in our origins and infinite in our final destinations.

I know I have not done full justice to the three cauldrons of life. Each of us will have our own connection and our own understanding.

Perhaps there should be mention of one other cauldron. This cauldron is perhaps the greatest of them all because it is within this majestic womb that all that is is held. The mighty Cauldron of the Cosmos with her outstretched arms holds hundreds and thousands universes, too many constellations to count and so many individual planets. So vast is her cauldron that we cannot comprehend it, and yet still we are held and nurtured, created and sustained, immortal within this primal mother's womb.

We are the sum total of all that has been before. The cauldrons are the primal instincts, the primal alchemic brew and the magic that flows through all of us, connecting us to the here and now but also ensuring that the origin of all things walks within us into tomorrow. It is through my craft and magic that I can make that connection, acknowledging who and what I am and drawing on that energy to focus my intent.

The craft is, in my experience, flexible but a hard task master. It demands time, dedication and a willingness to develop. You are forced to face yourself and see yourself for who you really are. This also means dealing with aspects of yourself that you don't like or that frighten you.

Instead of running from those fears, the tasks and demands that practicing the craft can incur we should remember that ultimately it is about looking at what works, what doesn't, what you like and what you don't. It is about setting realistic and achievable goals and in the process caring about yourself and learning to love yourself for who you truly are. It is about becoming the best that you can at any given time, using what ever gifts and talents you might possess. It is about life, living and being in the here and now to the best of your abilities.

Control dramas are patterns of behaviour created, learned or inherited which can dictate appropriate or inappropriate coping strategies. The will also define how we perceive ourselves as a consequence, as a victim, a control freak etc. However, they are often so indoctrinated in to our psyches that we often don't recognise them. When, finely we do recognise a specific pattern in our behaviour, we can struggle because we don't know how to go about changing it hence the advice that I was given "the best place to start is with yourself and what you don't know".

Don't worry if you don't actually own a cauldron, use a saucepan. I've used a preserve pan in the past. Just make sure it is heat resistant and fireproof. Then take that step over the threshold and trust yourself as you step into what can feel like the unknown. Allow yourself to connect with each of the cauldrons of life and immerse yourself with the different aspects of who you are and what constitutes your world. Don't worry about experimenting because that's how we find things out. Submerge yourself in the journey to each primal Mother and see what hidden wisdom, what treasures, what inspiration you find and don't be afraid of the fire in your head.

Samhain Night

It is the time of drawing in
And dancing around the fire
With a song in our heart of the summer that's been
At this most sacred of all rites.

Between, betwixt and all around
The darkness begins to fall
So stir the cauldron well and drink from her brew
On Samhain Night.

Remember the Crone and her promise of truth
That life always springs anew
For it is the time of no time
With thin veils and gateways through

So great all those who have gone before
And welcome them home
And know through the darkness you won't be alone
For in truth they are part of you.

Between, betwixt and all around
The darkness begins to fall
So stir the cauldron well and drink from her brew
On Samhain Night.

JOURNEYING INTO THE CAVE OF CAULDRONS

Part 1: The Journey
(Play back Part 1 taken from Chapter 1, or read out the transcript to assist you as you journey.)

Part 2: Into the Caves
As you reach the depths of the Cave of Cauldrons, think about the alchemy of your life. What do you want to manifest? What do you want to rid yourself of? This amazing cave is about life, death and rebirth. It is the womb, the universe, the place of growth and development. Know the potential you were born with, have already utilized and have yet to discover.

What is in your personal cauldron, if anything? What do you wish to start brewing so as to manifest it? Look about you, sit a while, see what happens, if anything. This is your magical place. What are the tools of your magic, the herbs of your knowledge and the essence of your spirit? All of these things and much more might be found within your cave. It is your cave so the truth and the detail will always lie with you.

Part 3: The Return and Awakening
Use the transcript provided in Chapter 1. Awaken from your journey happy and refreshed.

CERIDWEN'S POTION
Ceridwen brewed a potion in her cauldron for a year and a day, a spell of transformation, wisdom, knowledge and beauty, a spell of such magnitude that every ounce of her magical know-how was used. Once finished, this amazing potion was intended for her ugly and stupid son Afagddu.

But it was Gwion Bach who, whilst minding the sacred and powerful potion, managed to get three drops upon his thumb which he then placed into his mouth. Three precious drops of inspiration were all that was needed: it was enough for him to gain all the potion had to offer and it was enough to render the rest of the potion useless.

Ceridwen was beside herself with fury and rage and, believe you me, there is Ceridwen was beside herself with fury and rage and believe you me, there is nothing like a wronged and resentful goddess let alone a mother whose child has been robbed. So what commenced was an epic chase, a chase of shapeshifting from animal to bird and fish until finally to single grain of corn and a big black hen remained. Ceridwen the black hen devoured Gwion Bach who was now the single grain of corn, putting an end to his life...or so she thought, but instead nine months later she gave birth to the most beautiful and radiant of children, Taliesin, he of the Radiant Brow, Awen flowing through every pore of his being, so talented, so wise and so knowledgeable. He had been born, faced death, survived and been reborn transformed.

This is an inspirational story that depicts the transformations and changes in our lives. We may not have Ceridwen's powers of alchemy and magic but we have our own and she can be our inspiration, Goddess of grain, transformation, death and rebirth.

Ceridwen's Bath Potion

This is a recipe that you might like to try. It is my own Ceridwen's bath potion, a potion to fully immerse yourself in. Allow yourself to fully relax and contemplate, invoke and evoke the changes, transformation and the wisdom that you may seek.

Into a muslin bag place the following ingredients:

3 tbsp powdered milk
2 oz dried or 4 oz fresh elderflowers
A handful scented red rose petals
3 tbsp oats
2 oz dried or 4 oz fresh camomile flowers

2 oz dried or 4 oz fresh lavender flowers
A few drops of essential oil of rose or vervain

Tie the top of the muslin bag and place under the running hot tap as you run your bath. Experiment with what you want to put into your inspirational bath. The recipe I have provided is a suggestion; you may already have favourite herbs and aromatics which will resonate on a deeper and more personal level with you. Whatever you chose I am sure you will enjoy.

Chapter 12
THE CAVE OF THE SILVER SPINNER

I Am the Weave

I am the weave that time forgot
Spinner of sacred weft and warp
Knot work plaited in blessed threes
Singing and dancing in the evening's breeze.

I am the spider of the silver moon
She of the orchard and cauldron true
Spiralling eternally on silken thread
Intricate, so delicate are my woven webs.

I am the shapeshifter, the raven of the night,
Merging in balance both dark and light,
Brewing my spell of life anew,
For I am the Mather and this is my truth.

Weaver of the Sacred Web

Look into my eyes for they tell my story, falling further back into and through the kaleidoscope of light and time. Listen to my words and know they are but shadows of the experience, the essence and the knowledge of who and what I am.

All of you who claim to know me so well, think again, look harder…

Do you truly recognise me? Not many of you I'll wager, for all your proclamations and your willingness to face such truths.

Wipe away your tears my dears, they serve you nought. It is not your fault, this web I've woven. I will not give you that power. Perhaps you helped to shape its weave, but I alone made it. It is I and only I who adapted my precious web, sharing it, leaving it unprotected, unloved and in disrepair and gathering dust, hanging from the rafters.

I am as old as the sacred landscape and as deep as the eternal cauldron. Did I not spin the threads of time itself and weave the thrones of the Gods into being? And yet I forgot as I spun for others, I forgot my own web and the weaving of that web.

Yes my dears, spider I may be, but it is the role of the fly that I have played these many years, becoming trapped in my own silken threads, allowing some of you to feed upon my flesh and suck upon my spirit…oh yes, you know who you are. I am the Silver Spinner, my wheel forever turning, spiralling eternally on silken thread, intricate, so delicate are my woven webs.

The Sacred Tapestry of Life

During our lifetimes we weave rich tapestries of our own, as well as being part of the vastly larger one that is humanity and the world. Bright and colourful, the threads are woven together telling our story, remembering, recording and then passing down our personal piece of the universal tapestry to the next generation so that they might add their stitches.

As we are growing who do we dream of being? What kind of goddess do we envisage ourselves becoming, and what web do we see ourselves spinning? Is it positive or do we sink and cringe at our perceived inadequacies? We are not perfect; we are not blemish free without the scars of childbirth, freckles and spots, lumps and bumps of all sizes. We are not, for the most part, a size 0, nor do we resemble the pseudo image of the sacred feminine and womanhood depicted and manipulated by the mass media. Sometimes it saddens me that we do not accept our beauty and individuality, nor recognise ourselves as the Goddess manifest.

Perhaps it is symptomatic of the times we live in that we have stopped listening to ourselves. We must look into those deep places that are covered in shadow. Only in doing so can we truly are accept personal responsibility for who and what we are and the web that we weave.

How do we honour ourselves as women, our sacred feminine? The only 'honouring' seems to be in the quest to achieve the impossible, to have looks or a body other than the one we have, for example. We shy away from the true essence of our potential, our strengths and our absolute beauty in all its guises. Any 'honouring' is led by the powerful media machine and the modern gods of celebrity that it creates. This has gone into the pot along with aeons of conditioning regarding gender roles, with image and accepted behaviour set by the social norms, which in turn are set by an apparently unstoppable culture ruled by global media forces. This continues to affect the expectations that we place on ourselves and those around us. Things are changing slowly, but the sacred feminine is not fully understood, taught or given credence. The rich tapestry and the Sacred feminine is about our place within the cycle that is life. It weaves our potential, our magic, our craft, our wisdom, in essence our very being together for all to see, including the duality that is needed at different times in our lives. It enable us to stand on our own and in our power as we weave our intricate and beautifully personal webs, ensuring that as we do so we can be secure in the knowledge that we are held by the natural order of things.

How do we know the Goddess in all her natural guises? Look to yourself. Is she not, in truth, an extension of ourselves? Are we not the creator, the initiator, the Goddess manifested?

The sacred feminine is the source of who we are as women but it also shines within men. How many of us honour and revere this true aspect of the living Goddess? I do not view the sacred feminine as separate from myself (excuse me whilst I laugh at myself, I can't believe how sanctimonious that sounds). Although I understand the concept and many a time have spoken the words, I didn't always *truly* know it and I certainly didn't always practice what I preach. It is still not always an easy thing. Does this mean that I do not accept the Goddess as an external force, divine, ferocious and all-powerful? Of course I do, because everything is about energy exchange and she is me as I am her.

I have always found the ancient and sacred markings that our ancestors used to decorate their bodies, or the scars that they acquired through life and battle and then wore with pride and honour, to be fascinating. It would seem that this tradition can be found in many of the indigenous cultures of the world, used by both men and women. Each marking held meaning, its significance known and understood, telling a story, holding a dialogue with the Gods, offering protection, strength, courage and status, but also acting as a reminder and a natural diary of life's experiences. Many of us have tattoos, but what do they mean to us as individuals and as a tribe, community or nation? Have we earned them? Do they convey a message or record our stories?

I have no tattoos but my body is marked and scared, like many women who have the stretch marks of pregnancy, or operation scars. Is it not a sad reflection of our society that we have been conditioned to view such things as ugly, a form of disfigurement because our bodies are no longer pure and perfect?

I look at my body, round, soft, curvy, flawed by today's standards of beauty and fashion. My scars and stretch marks, silvery and long travelling up my midriff, are a map that tells part of my life story. They are my war-wounds, a reminder of all the battling I have had and remind me of the children I have given birth to. If we look at these markings as part of our personal web it helps to identify our personal magic; I can use my matrix to draw on the reality of who I am.

The DNA that is woven throughout my body is the inherited thread of my web and I am the manifestation of that. My power is in who I am and in all that I have experienced. I should honour all aspects of myself as they are part of my web. I have often joked that I could direct people to Scotland and back via my scars and stretch marks, but why don't I look upon them with pride? They are the evidence that my children were born, they tell the story of my life. They are the markings of achievement. The scars from my operations should remind me of my strength and endurance facing life threatening illnesses.

My body is not one of a youthful maiden, but I am in my forties and I have been pregnant six times, given birth to three children and I have had several major operations over the years. It is ridiculous that society expects us to remain forever young and against the natural cycle of life. I would like to be slimmer and manage to keep the wrinkles and grey hair at bay for a few more years, but this is me and my power is in understanding that the beauty in my web is in how I see it and the story that it tells is the story of who I am.

How many of you are now reading these words and thinking, yep... know where she's coming from; it doesn't have to be like this.

What do we have to say as women? Should we not embrace the beauty of knowledge handed down? Should we not embrace and embody all that we have learned, experienced and shared, empowering us to lift the veil that sometimes hangs between and yet always around us?

We dance and sing to raise energy, paint our bodies to honour and protect, all women together, powerful and glowing in the luxurious heat of the fire. We move in rhythm with the drum as we draw down the moon, with the tides of Mother Earth pulsing through our veins, the river of our blood flowing freely along with the ebbing and flowing waters that feed all of life.

But how can we within craft claim to honour the Goddess and the sacred feminine if we have no liking for ourselves and are led by the nose into buying into the concept that we are never good enough?

My web has weathered many storms over the years and although the aftermath has often left it in need of serious repair, on the whole it has remained intact, growing ever more intricate in its design and weave and therefore stronger.

It is not surprising that the spider, the ultimate weaver, is so important within the craft. I work with spider energy, weaving and mending, creating and protecting. Grandmother Spider is awesome in her abilities to stanch the flow of negative energies and physically to stanch the flow of blood with her spider-web - it acts as natural gauze allowing the wound to heal whilst still breathing.

Ironically, I am petrified of spiders in reality. If you are working with them as much as I do on an energetic level, you can be sure the real ones will always find you! They are the bringers of news and generally significant to the weave of life around me and those I know. Often, however, their message is sometimes lost as I pass out or have a panic attack. I have to smile to myself as I write this, because I know it is irrational, but it is very real.

A few years ago I facilitated a women only workshop. We were a mixed bunch of different ages and life experiences and yet most of us shared a common feeeling of being embarrassed, shy and uncomfortable with our bodies for various reasons. The aim of the workshop was about reconnection, to work with each of the main aspects of the sacred feminine and the Goddess in turn - Maiden, Mother and Crone - over three days. The intention was to identify and personally acknowledge the connection of the sacred feminine within, and look at ways in which we could then use that power on both an energetic level and in a ritualistic way. Each day we focused on one of the aspects of the Goddess and used our knowledge of who we are and our experiences to weave a web to make that connection energetically, ritually and communally. The weave of each woman's web was personal to them, spinning and manifesting the next phase of their lives whilst holding onto important threads and discarding those that were worn or broken.

On the third day, the day of the dark moon, we had our last gathering to prepare for the evening's grand final ritual honouring the Crone aspect and of course to recognise the wisdom of the Crone, which is understanding, regardless of what phase of our life we are in, that we are always all three aspects of the Goddess in one, the sacred feminine in its totality.

I should point out that not all of the women were used to ritual, craft or Druidry. For some these were totally new concepts and a different way of viewing themselves and the world around them. It was big for them, challenging all their pre-set ideas and conceptions.

As night fell, so did the rain. It was cold and wet, but undeterred we donned our robes and finery and made our way along the track, over a very dodgy bit of bridge that crossed the brook and up the hill to the grove at the top. We entered the grove in darkness and then set about lighting a fairly substantial fire. The sacred space was created, candles and lanterns were lit and finally, when we were ready, the drums began and the soft murmuring of singing and chanting commenced as each woman removed her clothing until we all stood in the darkness (apart from the glow of the fire) naked and exposed.

Singing and with drums beating, each woman's body was painted with beautiful designs such as spirals, leaves and flowers from head to toe. It was an amazing experience and showed trust within the group, women honouring women with love, kindness, creativity and inspiration. Then we danced, we drew up the energies from all around us and from each other, from the grove itself and from the fire.

Nemetonia, guardian of the sacred places and of groves, filled the air. We danced, we chanted, we invoked. The rain fell but we did not notice, the air was cold, but we did not feel it. We were liberated, free and in our power. Women of different ages, shapes and sizes, women who came from totally different backgrounds, joined together, empowered and immersed in their own magic, in their craft, honouring themselves, each other and the sacred feminine. Three days of work were brought together so that we, as women, could view and acknowledge ourselves as whole, not fragmented but strong, beautiful, powerful and understanding our personal weave and the unique and inspirational webs that we create and display to the world.

My body, although a shell on some levels, is the web of who I am, supported in time and space. It is what keeps me alive, attracts others to me or keeps them away. All of this, of course, depends on how I use my web and express myself through it. The spider within is my intellect, my inner hidden self. It is the spider that is responsible for the web which is its temple and its means of survival. A web is a thing of beauty; it takes time, work, skill and an inner knowing to create. We are no different, no less beautiful or complex and unique in our formation.

We are the creation of our parents, our ancestors and most importantly of ourselves, which is pretty bloody spectacular and impressive when you think about it. We are adaptable, versatile, strong and yet pliable. We can move through dance, by jumping, we can walk and we can run. We have the ability to be seen or unseen depending on where we are and how we stand. Our beauty, our individuality and uniqueness is no less staggering than that of the spider's web and just like the spider we too can harm, kill and trap those around us, regardless of our intent or because of it.

Should not each blemish, stretch mark and scar be viewed as a natural tattoo, a badge of honour and pride, telling the mysteries and the stories of our life experiences and of who we are? My body is an intricate web, magical, sacred and with purpose and that is a magic as old as time, powerful in its natural state of being because it is a natural part of what makes us who we are.

Weaving Magic
Weaving and knot work is one on the oldest forms of spell craft. From spinning the wool to knitting the garment and then wearing it, to sewing your stitches and patchwork, the patterns and the knot work, each is a spell of intent. For aeons knot work has been used as a means of honouring and protection. Our ancestors plaited their hair, a triple knot in honour of the triple aspect of the God or Goddess but also as a protecting spell.

Sailors' knots have a practical application of course, but the intent is protection. My dad told me that there are sayings that accompany most of the knots that are spoken out loud. Not tying your knot in the correct way aboard a ship could mean the difference between life and death in certain circumstances.

Aran knitwear, with its distinctive pattern, is a protection within the actual garment to ensure the fishermen came home safely from the sea. It was also used as a way of identification with each island using their unique pattern. As dad always said "The sea is a jealous mistress and will not be ignored or forgotten".

No matter our choice of working, we weave our web and sew our intent within it. Patchwork circles of women sat and created a work of art with meaning in its pattern, remembrance in its fabric and the intent of happiness, peace and fertility for the recipient of the item.

When women work together in circle it is a time of laughter, sharing, learning, ritual and gossip. Women bond and support one another, there is sisterhood and within that sisterhood the opportunity to creatively capture a piece of who they are.

I often introduce this aspect of craft into the workshops I facilitate when working with women. Many of us don't have the same support networks as others and often we have lost or forgotten the wonderful sense of being within a group of women, laughing, chatting, sharing, empathizing, supporting and supporting ourselves and just being.

This is not a new concept; it is as old as time itself. However, society today does not appear to have the same values, we have lost the extended family and in many cases we no longer live near to any of our immediate family and the hectic pace of modern life can take us over.

I have been lucky and have my children. I grew up in a family and extended family of strong women, women with a voice, assertive and very creative. The women around me taught me by example and through stories. I have fantastic memories of my mum and all my adoptive aunts (her friends) sitting around chatting, making things for us children, especially leading up to Yule. The laughter, humour and sheer energy was intoxicating. If grandma was around then the stories were bigger, more exaggerated and hilariously funny.

Of the other women in my life, there are three who have had an important role and have influenced me in ways that I feel are special and precious.

Thorney was just an amazing woman, creative, knowledgeable and gentle. From the age of eleven she was my dearest mentor, a second mum. She taught me so much I can't really put it into words. My love of herbs grew with her along with my love of the history of the ancient Britons and their tribes and eternal magic. She supported me throughout my life, encouraging me to be me and to write this book, and it saddens me greatly that she will never be able to read it.

Thorney was a quiet woman, unassuming, gentle and yet very talented with her arts and crafts, cooking and dress making. I loved the hours we spent talking about the different aspects of journey work, the medicinal properties of herbs and other healing disciplines. She supported and held me in some of the darkest days and years of my life and I cannot tell you how much I miss her counsel, her friendship and her love.

She was a natural wise woman of the Old Path. Her insight and understanding helped me so many times over the years when I struggled and lost my way. Her magic is still strong and her weave of intent still as powerful, but her focus was always on the needs of her family and others and seldom on herself. I love her with all of my being for her patience and her gifts of time and support; she was truly a special lady who was taken before her time, leaving all who knew and loved her with a space in their hearts which will always remain hers.

The second lady important in my craft development was my Aunty Ann, an outrageous woman, strong, opinionated, domineering, hilarious, generous and very challenging, a witch of the first order, clever and knowledgeable and very spiritual. Like most people I grew up influence by, Aunty Ann also is very eccentric and on some levels very much like grandma. (Blimey if she reads this I am in serious trouble!)

As a child Aunty Ann never seemed afraid of anything. As an

adult I know this not to be true but she protected me as I grew up and I could talk to her about anything; she was always interested and encouraged my love of divination. It has just occurred to me writing this that I have always assumed that it was Grandma who sent me my first tarot deck when I was twelve but in truth it could have been Aunty Ann. I had never thought of that until now.

The third woman who influenced me was Bonnie or Bone as we called her. She is the mother of my oldest and one of my dearest friends Berkeley. Inseparable, Sparks (Berkeley) and I pretty much grew up together. Bone was yet another important mother figure during my teenage years in particular. Long hot summers, picnics by the river and or the village green watching cricket, camps, custom and classic bike rallies and shows, parties, oh yes lots and lots of parties…Fantastic! It was bohemian, it was colourful and magical. We shapeshifted our looks and outward demeanour, New Wave, New Romantic, punk, gothic, elegant and beautiful, walking artistic creations. We were stunning and we were beautiful, we were young and we could touch the stars, what more can you ask for?

Bone taught me glamour with a capital G and how to use it on a bigger scale than the original lessons by grandma. She taught me to express myself, to believe in my abilities, dressing up, pageantry, celebration and ritual. A truly inspirational witch, a stunning artist to this day, full of creativity, Bonnie taught me to look beyond the obvious, to not get caught in the glamour of another, to see the world for all its potential but at the same time to not ignore the shadow and the darkness. She nourished that side of me that is the alchemist, the weaver, the ovate and the *Awenyddion*. Inspirational and awesome is the beautiful Bonnie Bel.

An amazing truth is found in the saying *what a tangled web we weave*. These women and those noticeable by their absences within these pages are all part of my weave and therefore part of my web.

So what are the practical applications of drawing on the power that is spun energetically within our personal web? A spider draws on all its experiences, its inherent knowledge and its belief and trust in its own instinctual senses. It is like any other entity; it is only interested in singing its own song. Spider does not waste its energy and life wanting to be anything other than what it is. Spider sings the song of spider and its power is undeniable and its skill and wisdom is staggering, if for no other reason than it is what it is.

We should do the same. Are we no less spectacular in who and what we are? Our inherent wisdom, our knowledge and our life experiences shape who and what we are, our personal weave and our personal magic. Our web is a manifestation of all these ingredients and our body, our outer shell, is our attraction, our personal designer brand label in its own display cabinet encouraging the outside world to come closer and explore the hidden and the unknown, and ultimately to meet the spider!

JOURNEYING INTO THE CAVE OF THE SILVER SPINNER

Part 1: The Journey
(Play back Part 1 taken from Chapter 1, or read out the transcript to assist you as you journey.)

This meditation is to enter the internal Cave of the Silver Spinner. Within we are eternally weaving the web of who and what we are, focusing on what we need, on all the threads that we have brought together from all of the other caves that represent the different facets of the sacred feminine that is personal to us.

We are the spider of the silver moon, we are the weavers of our own fates, we are the ones that hold the threads for others so that they may find their way. We are strong, we are survivors, we are creative. We are fierce when we need to be and we manifest our own reality. Just like the spider we can adapt and we can change our environment to ensure our continued wellbeing and ensure our web is maintained and representative of who we are at that moment in time, displaying with pride the sacred Goddess that we are.

Part 2: Into the Caves

Focus on your web, what it means to you and all that has gone into creating your web through the years. What condition is it in? Is it doing its job? Perhaps you are looking for guidance from the spinner. Look around the cave. What can you see, what can you sense, is there any other person there? What, if anything have you hung on your web over the years? Is it tired, broken and dysfunctional? Have you neglected to maintain and repair your web? Remember you are the spinner, and you are the creator. This is a place of sanctuary, it is the heart of you and where you are truly yourself.

Part 3: The Return and Awakening

Use the transcript provided in Chapter 1. Awaken from your journey happy and refreshed.

WEAVING A WEB OF INTENT FOR THE COMING YEAR

At Samhain, in my workshops, the women I work with are encouraged to make their own web. The aim is to externalise their inner web and renew their weave, creating a completely new web in some instances. The women sit in circle, chatting and sharing, but I ask them to focus their intent into their weave. The floor in the centre of the circle is full of beautiful and brightly coloured wools, ribbons and threads, and there are twigs, nuts, shells, beads, crystals and much, much more. Each weave represents an aspiration, a hope, a dream and affirmation - their personal intent however they choose to manifest it.

I chose to do this exercise at Samhain because it is the beginning and the end. The old year is devoured into the darkness of winter and yet at the same time we are at the beginning of a new cycle and our intent woven into our web can be nurtured over the winter months. Come spring, hopefully the new shoots will begin to grow, demonstrating the start and the implementation of our woven intent.

One of the things I love about the creating of a personal web is that it enables you to add and subtract at your leisure. The web can become your calendar and if you add seasonally to it can, if your intent is clear, empower you and act as a reminder to adhere to your hopes, dreams and aspirations and maintain the web that is hidden within. It is an uncomplicated but effective piece of craft that is a lot of fun to do on your own or as part of a women's circle.

I love to make things, to create my own magical tools and clothing. At the moment I am in the middle of knitting a hooded cloak for ritual wear. Knitting is one of the easiest forms of weaving and one of the oldest forms of spell-craft. You can weave and chant your spells of intent, protection and health etc. into the stitches as you knit.

Now I cannot sit here and tell you I am brilliant at knitting because I am not, but it doesn't matter, I love doing it and I find it calming and almost meditative. With the cloak I am making I am singing my charms as I go, directing my intent into my creation and when it is finished I will line it with silk and on the outside I will sew feathers and bones and add additional magical items that have significance to me. It will then be ready to wear and I will feel protected (and warm of course) and I will be ready to fulfil whatever commitment the ritual I am performing or taking part in requires.

I recommend having a go yourselves. I can't give you a pattern but I use a sort of plain knitting with lots of holes to give it a cobweb effect. Experiment, have fun and create something born of the cauldron.

Chapter 13
BEYOND THE BLOOD RED CAVE

Sacred moon and maidens true
In boughs of green and buds anew
Spring forth your seed in mists of dew
In faith of life from the Mother's womb.

Spirit woman, herbal healer
Weaver, Mother, all-knowing seer
Gather the threads of this tired land
Then patch and sew with magic's touch
Adding your blessings and charms enough.

Spirit woman, blessed Crone
Mystic, throw your runes and read your bones
Leave your sign in trees on high
Learn your wisdom from bird and beast
Remembering her secrets are there for all who seek.

So beat the drum and dance its tune
Priestess, shaman and Earth child too
Light the fire, embrace the flame
Life-giving energy, eternally warming
A seed of destruction if we ignore its calling.

All my life my craft has intertwined and woven itself around and through all that I am and all that I do. It is not a conscious thing. I do not need to think about it on a mundane level, it just is.

As we are creatures of this planet and part of nature, I believe that we all have a part to play in the cycle of life, death and rebirth. Each of us is unique and has our own gifts to share and own song to sing. So why do I feel as though we are still trying to play to another tune other than the one that is truly ours?

Our need to maintain and understand not only ourselves, but everything and everyone around us, is perhaps not only a natural human instinct and a tool of survival, but also part of a collective consciousness that links us to all aspects of the cosmos, seen and unseen. I believe our distant ancestors appeared to have understood this concept and consequently acknowledged their part within the 'great cycle', and so they created and built wondrous temples and shrines that honoured and (it is thought) celebrated our place within that never-ending circle of creation.

So yes I am a Druid priestess, I am a witch, I am an Aquarian with Taurus Moon and Scorpio rising. I am a dreamer, a visionary, I am a shaman and I am a healer. I am a mother, daughter, sister, lover and friend, I am creative, destructive, loving and hateful - I am all of these things and so much more, but first and foremost, I am a woman and I am an individual and as such I am still learning to embrace all aspects of who and what I am.

The titles, gifts and abilities are but aspects of me, natural and essential to my being and to my survival. However, the names themselves are but shadows, insomuch as by themselves they really don't mean much. They are names that for the most part are time specific, locality specific or conform to the acceptable face of the craft within our social norms.

Who you are and your personal preference will determine what name you call me but I see no difference. Craft is craft and a name is just that, a name and you will give it as much or as little credence as you wish, for as we know within craft intent is all.

I am what I am…with a healthy dose of glitter! For the most part you will see what you want to see and hear what you want to hear and sometimes only what I want you to see and hear. In truth it just depends on your personal preference, agenda and perception.

The craft is about survival and therefore life, the quality of that life and our place within the cycle of all things.

There is a message in all of us that needs to be shared and lessons that need to be learned. How we impart those messages to those around us and how we, in turn, learn the lessons that are shown to us may hold the key to our individual and collective humanity.

In writing this book I have asked myself why I want to do it and what I am trying to say. Truth be told, there is no easy answer to either of those questions. What I can say is not unlike (I suspect) a lot of writers, it has been a long and occasionally testing journey to reach this place, when I have felt unable to write anything down with any level of coherence. It has been a journey which has taken many twists and turns over the years, enriching my world in so many ways that now I feel that I might actually have something of interest to say and share with you.

Sometimes the journey has been joyful and at other times full of pain and sorrow, but always it has been a journey of insight and learning and I am absolutely sure that is the way that it will continue, as my journey has not yet reached its end.

Throughout, my love of magic, the hidden mysteries and rituals, the Gods and Goddess that together make up the rich tapestry that can be recognised as the indigenous spirituality of Britain have always been with me and I have never known any different. What has often been referred to as the 'eccentricities' of my family gave me my grounding and a solid foundation, allbeit quirky and colourful by most people's standards. From this I was able to move forward into adulthood. From that place I made my own way, which has been a varied, up and down sort of path, always extreme in where it has taken me (at least that's how it more often than not feels) and yet with a core that holds me in the understanding and connection with all that have been before me, my ancestors, my family, my community and my tribe, as well as the wisdom written in the landscape and the people that I have met along the way.

Because the roles and general perceptions of men and women have changed very much over the last few hundred years, we find ourselves in a position where we expect a lot of ourselves. We juggle so many balls between home, family, work and friends, throwing them all up in the air and expecting ourselves to be able to catch them every time without dropping a single one. Such high expectations are unrealistic and damaging long term. As a species we seem to have mastered the art of setting ourselves up to fail. We have doctorates in seeing the world, our lives, problems, other people etc. through rose tinted specs or bias glass. We are ultimately flawed beings, and that is okay. The key to facilitate us in moving forward in any given situation in a positive and pro-active manner is held in the personal responsibility of each of us and in the understanding of lessons learned. Once these aspects are embraced and implemented, it should enable both us and others to indeed move with hopefully greater ease along the path that is the ebb and flow of life.

Working within the Blood Red Caves is a direct connection to my ancestors, to the hidden wisdom and knowledge of the past that I feel is still relevant in the here and now. Working there is also ritual, a tool of personal development, a doorway into understanding yourself and the world around you and, just as importantly, it is about providing an opportunity to understand the reason why you are where you are in your life in the first place, empowering you to be proactive in your own personal development.

The caves can provide you with a focus on what you are trying to achieve with the connection and the intent to interact outside of your comfort zone. We are not fragile creatures who need continual bolstering and flattering to feed our egos and vanity. Where is our pride? Where is our true magic? Where are our mysteries?

The Cave of Glowing Embers

There is one cave to which I have not dedicated a chapter, not because it is of less importance than the others but because the Cave of Glowing Embers never leaves us and aspects of it are in all of the caves we have journeyed to throughout this book.

The Cave of Glowing Embers is the internal hearth fire of who you are, keeping you warm, igniting your passions and courage, fanning your fears whilst providing the energy that shapes your actions, your fight or flight in any given situation. It is the fire that burns with love and hate and all the spectrum of emotions that inspire or have disempowered you throughout your life. It is the essential spark of life that is required if life is to exist.

It is within the caves, as we continue our journey, that we will always find the Glowing Embers. We, and only we, have the power of construction and destruction within our lives. We will always be affected and influenced by others and circumstances outside of our sphere of influence but it is how we perceive ourselves within that rich tapestry which will decide whether this constitutes construction or destruction within the self imposed limitations and boundaries that we have surrounded ourselves with.

I have decided to leave the Cave of the Glowing Embers for you to find and explore. View it as an adventure, a place of nurturing and energising which can, if allowed, empower you as it feeds and keeps alive that eternal spark of individuality and uniqueness that is within all of us.

Windows into Souls

All that I have recounted I have taken from my journals. Within these pages I have shared some of my experiences into the Blood Red Cave and they are my magical reality, but we are all part of that cave and we all have our stories, hidden treasures and personal initiations that can be found there. To journey into the Blood Red Cave is a magical journey of personal empowerment enabling you to discover the hidden song of self.

Our journeys can resemble a shattered mirror that can distort the image; we can often delude ourselves or don't trust what we hear, see, touch or taste. In actuality all the fragments of mirror are doing is giving us a different image of ourselves, a different reality and a different aspect. They could also be representing other realms, dimensions or worlds or differing perspectives of us. Perhaps they are an outward reflection of what is within us that calls on our ancestral DNA, because they show us as we really are. We are many things to different people and apply ourselves differently depending on the need and circumstances. The real truth is that we never really see ourselves as others do and what we see in the mirror, especially a fragmented mirror, can often resemble images we don't like or recognise.

Maybe the magic, the craft and spirituality that enables us to journey into alternative realities and realms of being is a form science that is not yet fully understood and shows our liminality insomuch as our bodies are really only the outer shell, but we, in our true essence and form, are fluid and translucent. We are the mist hanging in the air, the breeze that floats on the leaves and the warm breath of a summer's night. We are all of this and more. Reality is a difficult concept but the brain doesn't differentiate between what is seen with eyes wide open and what is seen within our mind's eye. Both are valid realities and therefore both exist as we ourselves do.

Elizabeth I of England, when addressing her counsel of advisers and law makers in very difficult circumstances (a new queen in a male world, hostile to her being on the throne unmarried and the war between Protestant and Catholic raging) stated that she had "No wish to make windows into men's souls". Elizabeth was wise in her words, and nor should we. We can only look into the window of our own souls. We are only responsible for our own personal state of being. Very few things can ever be just black or white, but perhaps these colours define the infinity of potential within the Universal Cauldron and the tangible actuality of existence, knowing as we do, that all of creation contains the same elemental building blocks which brewed and then exploded all things into being. But within the black and white we cannot deny that there are definitely other colours in the spectrum. Perhaps it is these rainbows of colours that provide the shade and the detail and the spirit of being, so that when all the colours come together it is this that creates us, holds us, nurtures us and encourages us to move forward, never static, forever held within the eternal organic cycle and shape-shifting of life.

This is a poem I read recently by a lady called Debra Oakland and I identified with the sentiment and the strength in her words:

*I do not define myself by how many road blocks have appeared
in my path
I define myself by the courage I have found to forge new roads.*

*I do not define myself by how many disappointments I've faced
I define myself by the forgiveness and the faith I have found to
begin again.*

*I do not define myself by how long a relationship lasted
I define myself by how much I loved and been willing to love again.*

*I do not define myself by how many times I have been knocked down
I define myself by how many times I have struggled to my feet.*

*I am not my pain
I am not my past
I am that which has emerged form the fire.*

(Debra Oakland 2008 – Living In Courage)

I am not a person who is concerned solely with one particular aspect, the sacred feminine for example, to the exclusion of all else, but I am female and so by definition I see and relate to my world through the eyes, more often than not, of the sacred feminine. I make no apology for that but this is not a book just for women; there are aspects of the Goddess and the sacred feminine in all, including men. The nature of the caves is just as relevant to men. Their considerations and perspectives will differ, their priorities may differ as well - I do not know because I cannot see through their eyes, I am not living this world as a man.

Everything within craft is about adaptability, relevance and accessibility. It must be organic in growth and flexible and honest in its application. Mistakes are *allowed.* It is okay to mess up, to be flawed: *to ere is human,* the saying goes. It is through experience that we learn and it is through learning that we gain confidence and grow. I will never see the world through your eyes because I can never be you and you can never be me. Beautiful and amazing as we all are, perfection and beauty is, and always will be, in the eye of the beholder.

We should not be afraid to transcend ourselves. We should not be afraid to challenge ourselves and our own expectations of our self or of others. We should not be afraid to accept that we are inherently flawed as individuals and as a species. Instead we should remember and recognise that being flawed, making mistakes and even being afraid is still but a moment in time. A moment which might feel devastating and totally frustrating in its origins and yet, if we are able to take a step back and look through our own eyes differently, we will surely recognise that this is a moment that will be transformational in its nature and highlight our uniqueness, our courage, our wisdom and knowledge and our absolute beauty as we follow the labyrinth that is our personal journey *Beyond the Blood Red Cave.*